Your
Baby

Your
Baby

revised edition

Nancy Stewart

hamlyn

To Shawn, Leighton, Josie and Ben,
with thanks for joining us

First published in Great Britain in 1995 by
Hamlyn, a division of Octopus Publishing Group Ltd,
2–4 Heron Quays, London E14 4JP

This revised edition published in 2001

ISBN 0 600 60432 2

A CIP catalogue record for this book is available from the British Library.

Printed and bound in China

NOTE

While the advice and information are believed to be accurate and true at the
time of going to press neither the author nor the publisher can accept any legal
responsibility or liability for any errors or omissions that may be made. The reader
should always consult a physician in all matters relating to health and particularly
in respect of any symptoms which may require diagnosis or medical attention.

Contents

Introduction

The first 18 months with your baby are a journey of discovery, as you experience new feelings within yourself, develop new skills and understanding, and most importantly watch the emerging personality of the new and unique human being who has come to share your life. It is a time of wonder, and you may see the world with new eyes as you watch your baby growing and changing, beginning to make sense of the world, developing bonds of love, and communicating.

Being a parent is a huge and responsible job, and new parents need information about their role. *Practical Parenting* magazine regularly provides up-to-date information about babies, their health and development, and family life, in order to bring new parents support, provide useful tips from other parents' experiences, and help build confidence in being a parent. This book brings together information and ideas to provide a guide covering all areas of your baby's life.

Although you need accurate information behind your decisions about how to do things, in many ways your best teacher is your baby. Each baby is an individual, and what suits your baby and you may be different from every other. This book provides a framework of facts common to all babies, and suggestions based on the experience of other parents. It is offered as an ingredient for your melting pot of experience and your own baby's reactions, from which you will develop your own style of being a parent.

Having a baby also connects you in a new way with the vast human experience of one generation giving life to the next. I would like to thank all the parents who have shared their experiences with me. I am grateful, too, to *Practical Parenting* editorial staff for their help and encouragement with this book. Finally, my greatest acknowledgement is of course to my four children who continue to be my teachers, and to my husband John who is with me every step of the way.

N.S.

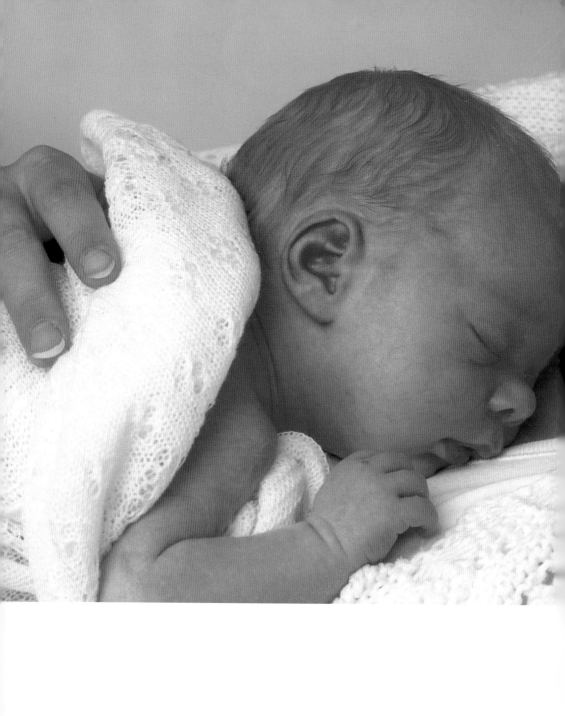

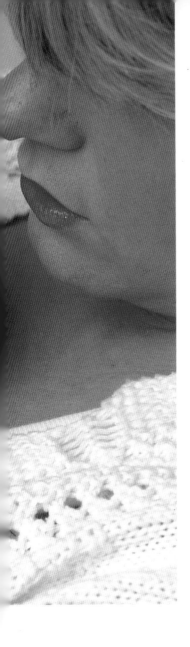

1

Meeting Your Baby

‘ *So there he was – this calm little baby with squashed ears. He seemed like a stranger instead of the baby I'd been living with for nine months. He looked really old and Dan said he looked like his grandfather. Over the next few days and weeks he seemed to grow younger and younger, as the wrinkles disappeared and his skin got soft and rosy.* ’

BECOMING A PARENT

Giving birth is a momentous experience and whatever sort of labour you have had, whether or not the point of it all entered your mind during contractions, its strength has been a marker of the enormous change in your life. A minute before, you were pregnant – and then suddenly you hold in your arms a new person who breathes, cries, squirms, watches and listens.

You have both just taken your first stride along the road of being parent and child. Your whole job as a parent could be summed up as helping your child to become independent – eventually, through all your love, support and teaching, becoming able to manage on his own. And the tall order for your baby is to grow up, from needing you for absolutely everything to becoming a fully independent adult.

Birth marks huge progress on this long journey. For the past months your baby has depended on you to breathe for him, eat for him, keep him warm and protected inside your own body. But now he is ready to begin taking on some of these things for himself.

TIME TOGETHER

You and your baby already know each other before birth. He has heard your heartbeat day and night and listened to your voice and felt the rhythms of your activity and sleeping. You have felt his kicks and wiggles, maybe even his hiccups, and are familiar with his quiet sleepy times. Fathers, too, may have been jabbed by a vigorous little knee or foot, and your baby may be familiar with the father's voice which has drifted into his world.

After the upheaval of birth, however, everything has shifted. Is this the knee you watched rolling under the surface of your skin? Is this the weight you have been carrying these past weeks? Now your baby has a face and, if you couldn't or didn't want to find out before from your scan, a sex, and is one definite person instead of all the possibilities that you could imagine before.

For your baby, it's all a new world. Air floods into his lungs, his skin is shocked by air temperature and then by strange textures; and lights and sounds are so much more intense than those he has known before. Instead of the steady pressure crowding and cradling his limbs in the womb, there is space all around him. He feels uneven pressures as he is lifted and held.

You both need time to absorb what has happened, and to recognize each other. The time immediately after birth is a time of heightened emotions and awareness, when you will want to examine and feel and marvel over your baby, and begin to absorb the fact that the birth is over and you are now a mother in a

' My first reaction was "Who is this? She's finally here!" I was so anxious to meet the child. It's like you've known a person by phone or writing and suddenly you see their face for the first time. There's that special look, like she knows you. ' FIONA

Your first moments with your baby will stay with you forever, however quickly she changes and grows. Though you've been expecting a baby over long months, holding this complete little person in your arms for the first time brings feelings you can never anticipate.

different sense. Having some quiet, private time together for parents and their baby is an important last stage of the birth.

Your baby, of course, doesn't understand what has happened, or even that he is one person and you are another. But in the midst of all that is new for him, he will be familiar with your heartbeat and breathing, your voice, and the feeling of being warm and closely held. So he will be comforted and reassured as you hold him in your arms and talk to him.

FIRST IMPRESSIONS

Your first eager inspection of your newborn may hold some surprises, since a new baby looks quite different from the rosy-cheeked cherubs a few months old that you see featured on baby products or congratulations cards. At birth, she shows signs of having just emerged from the watery environment of the womb. As well as being wet and slippery and possibly streaked with blood, being born has put your baby under pressure and stress, so she probably shows some effects of the birth process itself.

Head

A baby's head is large for her body – compared to an adult, it is proportionately four times bigger. At birth, the head may be pushed into an elongated

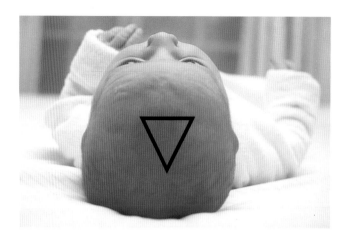

You might notice your baby's pulse beating in the larger fontanelle indicated by the triangle and see that it bulges slightly when she cries. If you ever notice the fontanelle bulging unusually, or sunk down, this can be a sign of illness and should be reported to your doctor.

shape, the forehead may seem short, or the head may be lopsided. This is the result of moulding, a process allowing the large head to change shape to come through the narrow birth passage safely. The effect lasts only a few hours and your baby's head will quickly become more rounded and even.

A baby's skull is not solid, but instead is formed of separate plates of soft bone joined by fibrous tissue. There are six soft spots, or fontanelles, which are the gaps between the bones of the head, but you will probably only be aware of the two main ones. The largest is a diamond-shaped area about 4 cm (1½ in) across, at the crown of the head. Behind that you might notice a smaller triangular soft spot. These soft spots will have closed up between the ages of about nine and 18 months.

There may be swellings on your baby's head which don't disappear as quickly as most of the effects of moulding. A large firm swelling of the skin caused by pressure during birth is called a caput and may take a few days to disappear. Or there may be an egg-shaped lump on one side of the head, actually a bruise on the outside of the skull. This is called a cephalhaematoma, and though it may take a few weeks to gradually flatten, it does no harm and will disappear without treatment.

If your baby has been delivered by forceps she may have minor bruising or shallow indentations on the sides of her head, while vacuum extraction may have left a swelling or red mark where the suction cup was applied. These marks will disappear within a few days.

Limbs

Alongside a newborn baby's large head and abdomen, her arms and legs may seem small and insubstantial. But you will probably be entranced by the perfection of the tiny hands and feet. A baby born at full term will have fingernails reaching to the ends of her fingers. Her legs will be slightly bowed, with her feet turned in, from having been curled up inside the womb.

Colour

At first your baby's hands and feet may appear pale or bluish while her trunk is pink, the result of her circulation not yet being efficient at delivering the blood to her extremities. Her immature circulation may also cause uneven colour in her body, with the top half pale and the bottom half red. Moving her position will sort it out.

Hair

Some babies are born with a thick crop of hair, while others are almost bald. The colour of your baby's hair may not be permanent, as it's common for the first hair to fall out in the early weeks and when new hair grows it may be a completely different colour.

There may also be fine body hair, called lanugo, often found over the ears, shoulders and down the back. All babies have lanugo in the womb, but especially babies born early are likely to have some still present at birth. It usually rubs off in a few days.

Skin

Your baby's skin will be covered with vernix, a creamy whitish substance which has protected her skin in the watery environment of the womb. It may be thick over much of the face and body, or be slight and appear mostly in the folds under the arms or elsewhere. The vernix continues to protect your baby's delicate skin in the first few days, so it's a good idea not to wash it off, but to let it be gradually absorbed.

Tiny white raised spots over your baby's face are called milia and are swollen or blocked sweat and oil glands in the skin, probably caused by the effect of hormones from the placenta. They are normal and will disappear before long, so don't squeeze them.

Skin-to-skin conact gives pleasure and comfort to both you and your baby, and is an important part of getting to know each other. Nothing speaks more directly than the language of touch, as you hold and stroke your baby.

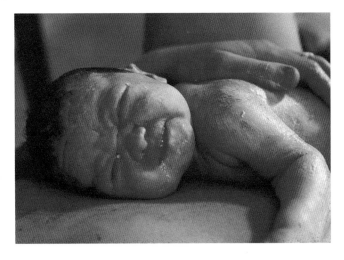

Dry or peeling skin at birth, usually on the hands and feet, is not a sign of eczema or other skin problems and should settle down after a few days.

Birthmarks

Many babies have small, flat red marks on the skin, most often on the eyelids, forehead and nape of the neck. These 'stork beak' marks are caused by the enlargement of tiny blood vessels and usually disappear over the first year.

Mongolian blue spots are uneven blotches of bluish colouring, usually on the lower back. They are most common on dark-skinned babies, and are caused by uneven pigmentation. They are harmless and will fade.

A strawberry mark may be present at birth, or appear after a few days. It is raised, red and soft, and will grow bigger over a few months. Although it may be unsightly, it will eventually fade and then disappear completely without medical treatment.

Eyes

Your baby's eyelids may be puffy as a result of pressure during birth. This swelling will go down in a day or two. There may be small spots of blood in the white of the eye, from tiny burst blood vessels, which will also soon go.

Almost all newborns' eyes are bluish-grey, because the pigment in the iris hasn't yet developed, although some brown-eyed babies have brown eyes from birth. Otherwise, it will be months before your baby's permanent eye colour will develop. When your baby cries, you won't see any tears. The tear glands only start producing tears after several weeks.

Mouth

Your baby's tongue may be anchored to the bottom of her mouth along most of its length. This won't affect her sucking and is no cause for worry. As the tongue grows, it grows mainly from the tip.

There may be tiny pale spots inside the mouth, along the gums and on the hard palate. They are small cysts, and will disappear without treatment.

Breasts and genitals

In both boys and girls, reactions to the mother's hormones during pregnancy temporarily affect the baby. The breasts may be swollen, and a few drops of milk may even appear. The swelling will disappear in a few days, as the mother's hormones are cleared out of the baby's system.

Genitals are also enlarged, and in girl babies there may be a clear or white discharge, or even a few drops of blood from the vagina as a result of the hormones. This, too, will stop naturally in a couple of days.

‘ *At first I felt relief that the baby's healthy and that everything's fine. They took him to do the Apgar checks so I didn't hold him for probably two minutes, but then the second I held him that was it – such joy.* ’ SHEILA

BONDING

How soon can you expect that your excitement and curiosity at seeing your new baby will become love? 'Bonding' is what we call the process of becoming so devoted to your baby that you happily take on all the responsibilities of being a parent over the months and years to follow. Human babies need more care for a longer period than any other animal, and the strong instinctive love of parents for their baby is the reason you give up your own sleep, take care of your baby's every need, and are prepared to put your own wishes second as long as your child needs you.

' An hour or so later my wife Peggy went to have a shower and one of the auxiliaries said "I'll take her through and put her in a cot now," and she was quite insistent. I said, "No, she's staying with me. She's my daughter." I think if she'd actually taken her off me I would have flattened her there and then. I'd talked to other fathers, but nothing prepared me for the powerful burst of emotions I'd feel, with this helpless little baby being suddenly all our responsibility. ' ANDREW

Early contact

The time immediately after birth can be an important stage in falling in love with your baby. For both parents, an emotionally demanding labour has suddenly given way to a new life, and the miracle of birth has an impact which opens the way naturally to strong feelings. Your baby, too, is especially open to meeting you in the hour or two after being born.

For one thing, both mother and baby are affected by hormones involved in labour and birth. Endorphins are one group of chemicals secreted by the brain, which are the body's natural painkillers and bring a feeling of relaxation and well-being. At birth, both mother and baby can have high levels of endorphins, which may account for the 'high' many mothers feel after giving birth. It may also be the reason that babies, particularly if they are not affected by the drugs used in labour, are likely to be calm and very aware for the period after birth. After this alert time, a baby will fall into a deep sleep and not have such a long quiet aware time again for several days.

Immediately after birth, the mother also begins to produce prolactin, another hormone involved in producing milk, and which causes you to feel relaxed and contented. This hormone, sometimes called the 'mothering hormone', may be involved in feeling that instinctive bond to your baby.

So the time right after birth is an ideal time for you to meet your baby – and it may be love at first sight. Many women experience a tremendous surge of love for their baby as they first hold her in their arms, feel her soft warmth, speak to her, and see her quiet gaze taking in everything around her minutes after her birth.

But though this time may become a memory that stays with you all your life, it is only one possible point for beginning to love your baby. Some women feel in touch with their babies as individuals during pregnancy and

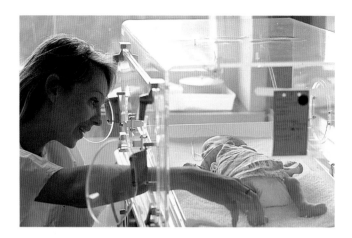

If your baby is in an incubator, at first you may be able only to stroke and talk to him, but just being there and helping in his care as far as you can will ease your worries and contribute in a way nobody else can to his progress.

already love them before birth. On the other hand, many women have little feeling for the baby in the beginning. It is very often two or three days before a mother feels love for her baby, and it's not rare for it to be up to two weeks.

Love needs to grow

There are many possible reasons for not having much feeling for your baby as soon as she is born. You may be physically and emotionally drained by labour, and not have the energy to respond to your baby. You may feel mostly relief that the birth is over, and want most of all to rest. The type of birth can affect your feelings – if it was long and difficult you may be upset or disappointed, or if much medication has been used you may feel groggy yourself, or your baby may be sleepy or irritable. Other issues in your life can cloud your feelings, such as problems with your partner or other children, money worries, or uncertainty about this pregnancy. Or it could just be that women react in different ways to the hormones that trigger maternal feelings, and for some it's a more gradual growth of that special bond.

There is no need to worry or feel lacking as a mother if you don't feel love right away. Bonding is not a once-and-for-all event that happens just at the beginning, but a growing feeling that develops as you and your baby get to know each other. For mothers who miss out on early contact, perhaps through either mother or baby having been ill, or for those who have adopted babies, the love that grows will be just as strong as for those who got off to a quicker start.

The most important things you need to encourage love to grow are enough time together, and privacy. You need time away from the distractions of other people and other responsibilities to watch your baby, talk to him, and have a lot of physical contact. Babies are naturally appealing, with their big eyes in a tiny face, soft warm body and scent which arouses your maternal instincts. Love is a two-way street, and your baby will be playing his part by watching you, especially wanting to look into your eyes, and within days he will respond specially to your voice and your smell and be comforted by you.

Occasionally a mother will continue to have dampened feelings for her baby. This doesn't mean that you're a bad mother or that you are necessarily suffering from depression, but simply that it's taking you a little longer to bond with your baby. But if you are worried about your negative feelings do discuss them with your GP or health visitor.

SPECIAL CARE

Most babies born at full term are fit and well. But in some circumstances, a baby needs special medical care from birth. Babies who weigh under 2.5 kg (5 lb) are considered small, and may need help and careful supervision in the early days. Some babies are small simply because their parents are small and they are fully mature and need no extra help. But most small babies are either small-for-dates (of low weight for the age because not enough nourishment reached the baby through the placenta), or premature (born early, so that some body systems may not yet be mature enough to function effectively).

Both small-for-dates and premature babies may have difficulty in maintaining their body heat, and because of low sugar reserves they must be fed frequently and blood sugar levels must be monitored. Particularly with premature babies, there may be breathing problems so the baby needs to be in an incubator with extra oxygen and warmth.

In some cases, it may be possible for a special care baby to be in an incubator beside your bed. But a baby who is quite ill or needs extra help will need to stay in a special care nursery. There the monitoring equipment and expert staff can keep a close eye on your baby and adjust treatment as necessary.

Parents' reactions

It can come as quite a shock if your baby requires special care at birth, and can't be with you. If your baby has arrived early, you may not feel ready emotionally, let alone practically. You will also feel anxiety about your baby's condition, and perhaps feel guilty that in some way you have let your baby down because you cannot look after him by yourself. Going through strong feelings like these, or even anger at the staff, your partner, or the baby, is part of adjusting to the reality of your baby having difficulties.

Seeing your tiny baby surrounded by high-tech equipment, with wires and drips and attended by efficient and expert staff may also make you feel out of place and useless. But your role in helping your baby is still central. Medical staff will encourage you to spend as much time with your baby as you can, and your presence, touch and voice will give comfort and strength to your baby.

If you have other children at home, or are released from hospital before your baby, the pressures of going to the hospital to be with your baby can be very great. Do enlist any help you can from relatives or friends to support you through this difficult time. Once your baby is stronger and you are able to hold and feed him, and eventually take him home, lots of cuddling and holding will build your confidence and help make up for his shaky beginning.

MALFORMATIONS

When a baby is born with a physical malformation the first reaction is often shock and even disbelief. Anger, guilt and sadness may follow quickly.

Accurate information is essential to limit worry as far as possible and provide the facts about the baby's prospects and possible treatment, including whether and when an operation will be necessary. In the initial shock of the discovery, parents may not take in what they are told, so repeated chances to ask questions and be kept informed are important. As well as medical staff, there may be a counsellor available at the hospital to help parents with the situation. There are also special support and information groups for the more common malformations such as cleft palate or Down's syndrome.

The fact that the baby is not perfect can at first overshadow everything else. But the baby as an individual will soon shine through, and as parents come to terms with the problem they can love their baby for the unique, special person he is.

POSTNATAL TIPS

◆ *When you hold your newborn remember that although she looks fragile, she is in fact very sturdy. Knowing she won't break, you will hold her more easily and without tension so she, too, can relax and feel secure.*

◆ *She needs you to support her head in holding or lifting her, because her neck muscles aren't yet strong enough to take the weight of the head.*

◆ *As long as all is well, your time together after birth needn't be interrupted for routines. Ask for weighing and measuring to wait until you are ready, and initial checks can be done with your baby in your arms.*

◆ *Try putting your baby to the breast in the hour or so after birth. She may not be interested at first, but if not try again. Getting started in the first period after birth is a good boost to successful feeding.*

◆ *Take some photos of your first meeting with your baby. She will change almost from moment to moment in the first few days, so you'll value the reminders.*

◆ *Even if you are tired after the birth, you may be too excited to sleep and need to relive everything in your mind. Having your baby with you to cuddle, or to see and feel peacefully sleeping, will help you absorb what has happened.*

QUESTIONS AND ANSWERS

Q: My baby's breathing is irregular. He breathes very fast for a while, and then sometimes it seems he's hardly breathing at all. Is there something wrong with him?

A: It is normal for a young baby to alternate between panting, fast breaths and shallow breathing. He will be about three months old before it settles down into a more steady rhythm. A newborn baby breathes about twice as fast an adult. He may also have snuffling sounds because his air passages are so small, or have hiccups which can look alarming as they shake his whole chest but which don't bother him at all.

Q: Is it all right for a baby to be delivered on to the mother's tummy and cuddled straightaway, or does the baby need to be wrapped up first?

A: A new baby loses heat easily, so it's important to keep him warm. The baby could be dried and wrapped to maintain body heat, but it is possible to have skin-to-skin contact with the mother and still keep the baby warm. If the baby is held against the mother, and then covered with a warm cloth, the mother's body heat will keep the baby warm and the baby will appreciate the body contact. Babies lose most heat through their head, so draping a cloth round the head prevents the baby cooling too much.

Q: My baby smiled in her sleep when she was just two hours old. Was this really smiling, or just a chance movement?

A: Some people would say it wasn't a 'real' smile, because it wasn't a smile done on purpose in response to something. It will be some weeks before your baby smiles at you on purpose. But early smiles like your daughter's seem to come when the baby is contented and relaxed, such as just drifting into sleep, and they probably are instinctive signs of pleasure or just feeling good.

Q: Since my baby's hands and feet are a bit blue because of his circulation, how can I tell if he is cold?

A: You can check his body heat by feeling his back or tummy. If they feel about the same as your own, he is all right. Don't worry about hands and feet being a little blue or pale in the early days, but if the lips or tongue look blue, tell your midwife or doctor.

Q: I put my baby to the breast soon after birth and he sucked well straight away, but I know there won't be any real milk yet. He's a big baby, so will he be hungry before my milk comes in?

A: Although regular breastmilk isn't produced right at birth, when your baby sucks he does receive colostrum. This pre-milk is especially rich in proteins as well as important antibodies, and even though there may be only small amounts it will sustain your baby very well until your milk comes in. Because it has less fat than mature milk, it is easier for your baby to digest. Keep putting your baby to the breast so he has the colostrum, and his sucking will encourage the milk to come in and make a smooth transition to mature breastmilk.

2

The First Week

' The first few days felt like magic, and I wanted to slow them down to hold on to it forever. She still seemed only half real, not quite in the same world as the rest of us because she was changing so fast. I could sit by the hour, just watching the expressions move over her face. '

BASIC NEEDS

As soon as your baby is born, the automatic care you had given her in the womb – feeding her and dealing with her wastes, keeping her warm and protected, with a cosy place to sleep – is exchanged for having to consciously provide for her needs. It may seem a daunting responsibility. But in fact your baby's basic needs are still very simple, and as long as they are met she is not very particular about the details.

So take your time over the first few days to settle in, and learn together. Get to know what your baby can do, and what she responds to. You may be amazed by how quickly she learns, moving from the first instinctive suck so that the first feed seems almost by accident, to calming down at the sound of your voice and getting ready for the feed she has learned to expect as you hold her in position. She will be using all her senses to learn about this world she has come to, but the most important discovery of all is that it is a safe place where she will be cared for and loved.

Warmth

A new baby has little body fat to keep him warm, and can't react to changes in temperature as fast as an adult, to maintain a steady body heat. The room temperature should be warm, around 21°C (70°F) for the first few days, and

Early checks by health care staff will monitor your baby's progress, including basic functions such as breathing and maintaining body heat, and weight and physical condition. If you have any worries your midwife will be glad to talk them over with you, explaining the usual progress over the first few days, and consulting a doctor if she feels it is appropriate.

the baby should be kept out of draughts. Your body makes a perfect heater, so your baby will be warm and comfortable snuggled in with you.

Food

Hunger is a new sensation for your baby and the need to be fed is so important that he feels it as an urgent pain if food isn't provided immediately. So he will cry loudly and insistently, and become frantic if he isn't fed quickly. It needn't come to that point, however. He will almost always wake hungry, and if you offer a feed when he wakes and stirs he won't have to become upset in order for food to arrive. He will then go smoothly from being asleep to being awake and satisfied, and he will be learning to trust life, and you. Don't worry about changing your baby until after he is fed – most young babies fill their nappies as a reflex during a feed so you would have to change him again afterwards anyway, and there is no point delaying the feed and having him get upset while you change him.

Sleep

Most new babies sleep a lot of the time, between around 16 and 20 hours a day. Your baby may have no appreciation of day and night, and be most wakeful and active at night, which is exhausting for you. You can encourage the idea that nights are for sleeping by keeping everything darkened and quiet for the night-time feeds. In the daytime, don't worry about keeping things quiet. Though sudden loud noises will startle and may wake your baby, he is used to a lot of steady rumbling and thumping noises in the womb, and won't be bothered by ordinary noise. It will be easier as he grows older, too, if he is used to sleeping through household noises from the beginning.

Physical contact

Touching, and being held, is another of your baby's basic needs. He has gone from the totally surrounding contact of the womb to the frightening emptiness of space, and he is reassured by being held in your arms, by movement, and feeling the familiar rhythm of your breathing and heartbeat. As you hold him, be sure you are comfortable yourself, because if you feel tense and awkward in the position, he will too. As long as his head is supported, and he feels securely but gently held, he will relax.

When you go to pick him up, talk to him and touch him to let him know you are there, so he won't be startled by sudden movement. Raise his feet slightly with one hand to enable you to slide the other under his body to support his back and head. Then, with one hand under his back and head, and the other under his bottom, pick him up as you continue to talk to him. In putting him down, keep your hands supporting his head and bottom as you lie him down and then slide them out. (See page 24 for ways to hold and handle your newborn baby.)

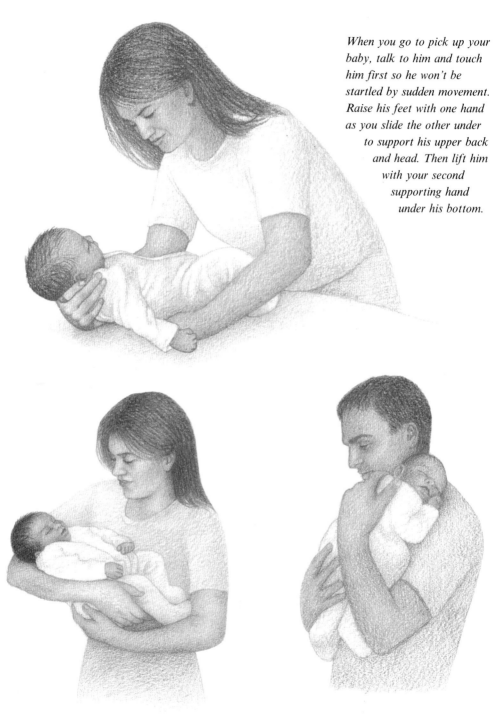

When you go to pick up your
baby, talk to him and touch
him first so he won't be
startled by sudden movement.
Raise his feet with one hand
as you slide the other under
to support his upper back
and head. Then lift him
with your second
supporting hand
under his bottom.

Your baby's head is supported and she feels
secure when cradled in your arms.

A baby enjoys your movement if you walk
about with his head resting on your shoulder.

24

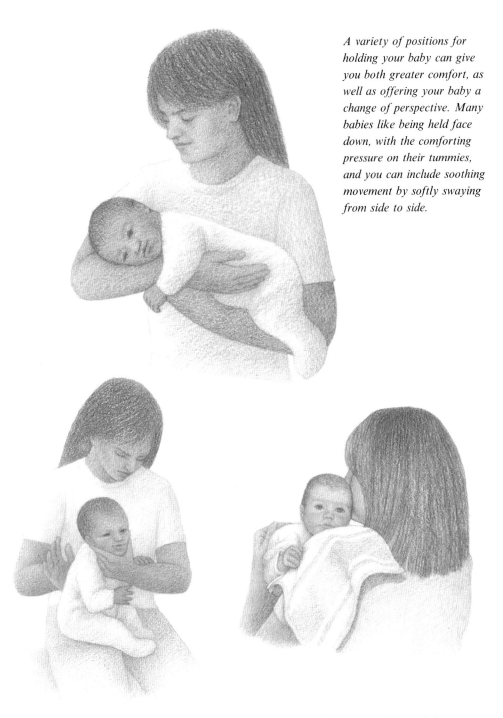

A variety of positions for holding your baby can give you both greater comfort, as well as offering your baby a change of perspective. Many babies like being held face down, with the comforting pressure on their tummies, and you can include soothing movement by softly swaying from side to side.

Help your baby to bring up wind by rubbing her back as you hold her on your lap.

Alternatively, you can hold your baby against your shoulder to burp her.

REFLEXES

At first most of your baby's activity is by reflex, an instinctive action that happens automatically in response to stimulation. There are some basic reflexes that are vital to life, such as the breathing reflex, the automatic emptying of bladder and bowel and the hunger reflex that makes her demand food. As she grows and matures, more of her behaviour comes under her control, instead of being a reflex.

Other reflexes you might notice are blinking and closing her eyes against bright light, and pulling away from a painful sensation. Some reflexes found in a newborn baby will disappear after a few months.

Sucking reflex: Your baby will automatically suck on something placed in her mouth, and may even have practised in the womb by sucking her thumb. A good sucking reflex is important for early feeding. In premature babies the sucking reflex may be delayed, so tube feeding may be necessary at first.

Rooting reflex: If you brush something against your baby's cheek, she will turn her head to that side and open her mouth. This is called the rooting reflex, and helps her to find the nipple (see page 55).

Grasp reflex: Your newborn baby will grip your finger if you touch his palm (see pages 20-1), and his grasp is so tight that he can support his whole body-weight if you lift with one of your fingers in each of his hands. This reflex, probably a remnant of prehistoric times when a baby needed to cling onto his mother, also applies to the soles of his feet which curl up when stroked, and disappears in a few months. He has to learn to grasp something on purpose.

Startle reflex: If your baby is startled by a loud noise or sudden movement she will react with her whole body, in the startle or Moro reflex – flinging out her arms and legs as if to grab something, throwing her head back, opening her eyes wide and perhaps crying (see illustration on opposite page).

Crawling reflex: If you place your newborn on her front, she will assume a crawling position since her legs are still tucked up towards her body as they were in the womb.

Walking and stepping reflexes: If you hold your baby upright so her feet touch a hard surface you will see the walking reflex, where she moves her legs as if walking forwards. If her shin touches something, she will raise her leg as if to step over it. This walking reflex will disappear and is totally different from purposeful walking which she will master only many months later.

SENSING THE WORLD

Your baby is highly aware and sensitive, so while you are watching him and discovering all that you can about him, he is experiencing the world around him, including the part that attracts him most – you. His instinctive interest in you is his part in the bonding process, and helps get the communication between you established.

Much of your baby's early activity is by automatic reflex, such as the startle reflex in response to sudden loud noise or movement, where the arms and legs are flung out wide as if to catch hold of something, eyes open wide, and the baby may cry.

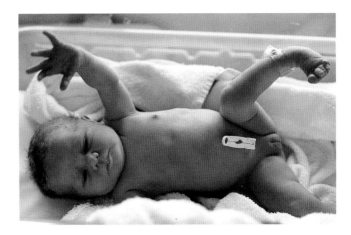

Sight

A newborn baby can see quite well, with a clear focus on objects about 25 cm (10 in) away and a more blurry image of things further off. So when you hold your baby in your arms and he looks at you intently, he is seeing you clearly. New babies show a preference for looking at a human face over any other shape, especially concentrating on the eyes. Eye contact is an important part of communication between people, so when he seeks out your gaze it helps you feel connected to your baby. Within about 36 hours after birth, your baby can recognize the shape and outline of your own face and will prefer to look at yours rather than others. He will also follow you with his eyes as you move.

Babies see colours and patterns, and prefer curved lines to straight ones, three-dimensional objects to flat images. In the early weeks, they're often more attracted to patterns in black and white rather than colour.

Hearing

Hearing is well developed, and even before birth your baby has been listening to your voice as well as many other noises. Because your voice is familiar, he will respond with greater interest when you speak. By only the third day of life, a baby will turn to the sound of his own mother calling his name rather than other voices.

Most mothers instinctively use a more high-pitched, soft, cooing voice when speaking to their babies, and in fact this is the voice range which a new baby hears best and prefers. Your baby also instinctively responds to human speech and will subtly move his body in rhythm with the speaking.

Taste and smell

Both taste and smell are highly developed senses. Your baby prefers sweet tastes, such as breastmilk, and by one week of age he can distinguish the taste and smell of your milk from the milk of other mothers. He is attracted to the milky smell, which he soon recognizes and which helps him to settle into a feed, and he is also attracted to his mother's body smell. He will, though, turn away from an unpleasant odour.

Touch

The skin and awareness of touch are the first sense organs your baby developed, and he is learning about the world around him through all the new sensations of temperature, pressure and texture. As you handle your baby, stroking, swaying, rocking, and cuddling, you are getting to know each other in a unique way, since touch is in some ways the most direct language between people.

MINOR WORRIES

Newborn babies are prone to a number of minor ailments, which can give rise to concern in the parents if they are not prepared for them. Here are some of the most common ones.

Navel

When the umbilical cord has completed its job at birth, it is usually clamped about 2.5 cm (1 in) from the baby's abdomen and then cut. After about 48 hours, the cord stump has shrunk and the clamp can be removed. During the first week after birth the stump continues to shrivel, while bacteria soften the base so that the cord finally drops off, any time from four days to six weeks later, leaving the navel.

The cord should be kept clean and dry, but gentle washing with warm water twice a day is sufficient. Antiseptic cleaners will only slow down the process of the cord dropping off. You can gently pull on the stump to clean in the gutter around the base. After the first day, a tiny bit of bleeding from around the stump is not a problem, but if the area around the stump looks red there could be an infection, so tell your midwife or doctor.

Vomiting mucus

A lot of mucus may be produced by your baby's stomach as a reaction to the birth, and she may vomit it up in the first day or two. It may be bloodstained and may make your baby uninterested in feeding. It may also briefly get in the way of her breathing, but she has a strong cough reflex and will clear it out of the way. Just lie her on her side if she needs to cough it up.

'*A funny thing happened when I went into the hospital to see them the morning after the birth. I walked onto the ward and heard my baby cry, and I immediately knew it was her – I didn't even have to ask the nurse. I recognized her cry straightaway, and I'd only been with her the previous night for maybe three hours.*' PETER

Sticky eyes

Many babies develop a discharge from one or both eyes in the days following birth, which may cause the eye to run or have sticky matter in it. The lids may even be stuck shut after a sleep. Your doctor should have a look at the eye, but it is very rarely conjunctivitis, an eye infection that could be passed on to the other eye or to anyone else. Instead, it is probably a blocked tear duct.

'I just loved the first weeks when he was a tiny, tiny baby, so vulnerable and so completely dependent. In some ways, though I know it's not quite true, I thought "I'm the only one who can do it". I felt so proud and thought, "Gosh, he's so pretty!" I think all mothers think their babies are pretty.' JANE

The tear ducts are tiny tubes which run from the corner of the eyes, collecting the tears which are constantly being produced to keep the eye moist, and passing them down into the nose cavity. In small babies, there can be a blockage at the bottom end of the tear duct, so there is a moist site where germs can grow, causing the discharge. A blocked tear duct needs no treatment, because it will almost always clear by itself. If a baby still has a blocked tear duct at six months, treatment by an eye doctor would be considered.

While waiting for the duct to become unblocked, clean the eye, using a piece of cotton wool dipped in cooled boiled water. Wipe from the outer edge of the eye into the inner corner, and use a clean piece of cotton wool for each eye. Your doctor may prescribe some antibiotic drops, which will not cure the problem, but may limit the stickiness while the body clears the blockage.

Squint

A lack of muscle power to control the eyes may make your baby appear to squint, especially when she is relaxed and feeding. As her muscles develop, she should be able to focus both eyes together by about three months.

Snuffles

A young baby may sound snuffly in her breathing, the result of small air passages rattling with extra mucus. The nose produces this mucus to protect the delicate nasal lining from milk which she may get into her nose in the early days. It doesn't mean your baby has a cold. If she did, she would also have a temperature or seem unwell in other ways.

Rashes

Skin is not a barrier as we sometimes think, but a living organ which absorbs many substances. Rashes in the early days are probably harmless signs of the skin reacting to its new environment. Your baby's skin may react to its first contact with clothing or other substances by producing a red, blotchy rash with small white or yellow centres. The weals look like nettle rash, and may come and go quickly on different parts of the body. The rash will clear up after a couple of days and needs no treatment.

In hot weather or if your baby is overdressed in any weather, she may develop a heat rash, tiny red spots which spread in the areas where the baby sweats – most often the face, neck, shoulders and chest, especially in the creases. Rinsing off the sweat will soothe the skin, but most importantly, make sure you are not overdressing your baby or using too many bed covers.

Dry skin

Most babies have dry, peeling skin a few days after birth as the top layer of skin which has been in contact with the amniotic fluid is shed. It needs no treatment, although you could rub on a little good-quality oil such as almond.

Pink-stained nappies

A pink stain in the nappy is probably a concentration of urate crystals from the baby's urine and is normal. With a girl, there could be a little blood from the vagina as a result of the mother's hormones, which will stop in a few days.

Jaundice

Many newborns develop a yellow tinge to the skin and in the whites of the eyes on day two or three. This is known as physiological jaundice, and is a result of the immature liver not being able to process and eliminate bilirubin. Bilirubin is produced in the breaking down of red blood cells. This goes on continuously in the body as red blood cells reach the end of their life span, but especially in the first few days because your baby needed more red blood

LOOKING AFTER YOUR NEWBORN

◆ *Try making faces at your baby. From the very first day, she will be able to watch you carefully and then copy you if you repeatedly stick out your tongue.*

◆ *Nights will be much less tiring for you if you keep your baby's crib or cot within easy reach of your bed.*

◆ *Change your baby after a feed, not before. Then she won't have to wait and get upset, and she will probably need changing afterwards anyway. When she's older and can wait for her feed, you can change her first so she is comfortable.*

◆ *Some babies feel more secure and sleep more soundly if they are swaddled, wrapped snugly in a cloth or shawl (see page 91).*

◆ *Whatever sort of nappies you decide to use later, newborn size disposables are handy for the first few days.*

◆ *Talk to your baby – it doesn't matter what you say. Don't feel silly if you find yourself using a high-pitched 'babytalk' voice – it will be just right for your baby, and she will love it.*

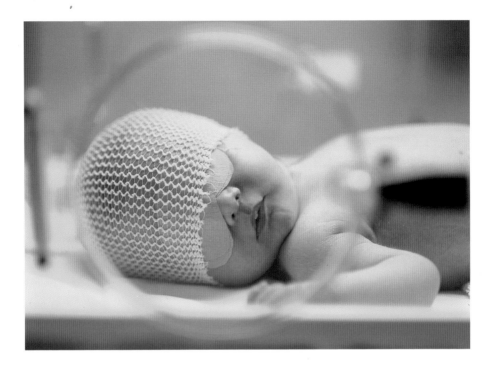

cells to carry oxygen before birth than he does now that he is breathing for himself. Because the liver doesn't excrete the bilirubin efficiently, it builds up in the bloodstream, producing the yellow colour.

Though it can be distressing not to hold your baby except for feeds, phototherapy can usually be provided beside your bed so you can still touch and talk to your baby.

The bilirubin level usually peaks at about day four or five, with the baby remaining alert and feeding well, and nothing needs to be done. If the amount of bilirubin were to reach very high amounts, though, it could be taken up by the brain and cause damage. So your midwife and doctor will keep an eye on your baby's colour and may arrange a blood test if they suspect jaundice. Treatment would be started long before damage could occur. The treatment is called phototherapy and involves exposing the naked baby, with pads to protect her eyes, to ultraviolet light.

MEDICAL CARE

As soon as your baby was born, he will have been given a quick check to see that his breathing is established and there are no immediate problems. At one minute after birth, and again at five minutes, an Apgar score will be recorded as a measure of how well he is managing the transition to life outside the womb. The Apgar score is a quick method of giving up to two points each for heart rate, breathing, muscle tone, body colour and reflex response.

Physical examination

Sometime later, when you and your baby have rested, a doctor will give him a more thorough physical examination. If your baby was born in hospital, this examination will be made by a paediatrician, and repeated when you are ready to leave the hospital. If your baby was born at home, your family doctor will usually perform the examination.

As well as a careful observation of your baby, the doctor will measure his head circumference and check the fontanelles, eyes and mouth. She or he will examine the abdomen and listen to the baby's heart and breathing.

Your baby's hips will be examined to check the condition of the joints. Many babies have 'clicky hips' because the ligaments are loose, as a result of pregnancy hormones the baby was exposed to in the womb. But a few babies are at risk of developing an abnormally shallow hip socket (congenital dislocation of the hip), which if not treated leads to a permanent limp and difficulty in walking.

The doctor will also examine the baby's genitals, and in boys will see whether both testes are in the scrotum. The testes are formed in the abdomen, and usually come down into the scrotum before birth. But sometimes one or both has not yet descended, and they can also go up and down at first. If the testes are not in the scrotum, the doctor will make a note to keep an eye on it.

During the first week, the midwife will take a drop of blood by pricking your baby's heel for the Guthrie test. The blood sample is then examined for very rare genetic conditions where the baby is unable to break down nutrients or unable to use them properly in the body. Other tests may also be done on the blood sample, to detect conditions such as thyroid malfunction and cystic fibrosis.

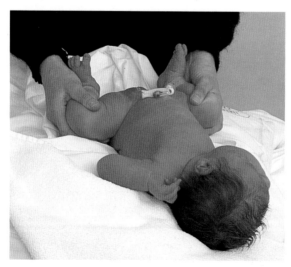

All babies are examined for congenital dislocation of the hip. If discovered before the age of six months, an affected baby can be fitted with a harness to wear which holds the hips up at right angles to the body, preventing the baby from stretching out her legs. After about 12 weeks the harness can be removed, and a deep hip socket will have formed, leaving the hip joint normal.

QUESTIONS AND ANSWERS

Q: My baby weighed just over 8 lb when she was born, but the midwife said she would probably lose some weight at first. Why is that?

A: Most babies do lose some of their birthweight before starting to gain weight again, and losing about 227 g (½ lb) or even up to one-tenth of the birthweight is considered normal. Most of this loss is fluid, because in the first day or so your baby may not have much interest in feeding, while her urine output stays normal. And it may be two or three days before your milk production is established. Not all babies lose weight, however, and if yours is born hungry and spends a lot of time sucking over the first 24 hours, your milk may come in more quickly and she may not lose weight.

Q: Even after a feed, my baby keeps making sucking movements with his mouth and he is restless and doesn't settle to sleep easily. Should I give him a dummy?

A: Starting to rely on a dummy right away isn't a good idea, especially if you are breastfeeding, because the time your baby spends sucking on the dummy might be more important spent at the breast to establish feeding. A baby sucks for comfort as well as for food, so there is no harm in letting him have a longer time at the breast even when you think he is not hungry. It may well settle him to sleep. Or you could try holding him, or swaddling (see page 91), when he is restless.

Q: My baby's cord has fallen off, but there is a bulge under the navel that comes out more when he cries. Is something wrong?

A: The swelling is an umbilical hernia, which is fairly common in babies and not dangerous. The gap in the muscle wall of the abdomen where the cord came through has not closed up fully, and so the contents of the abdomen push through, especially when the pressure is raised by crying or coughing. It is not painful for your baby, and nothing needs to be done. Almost all umbilical hernias close up by themselves before age five.

Q: Will a baby be spoiled if you pick her up when she cries?

A: It's not possible to spoil a new baby. In fact, it's been found that babies whose mothers go to them right away instead of leaving them crying soon cry less and are easier to comfort (see pages 98-9). She is crying because something is wrong, not because she wants to manipulate you. If you can solve the problem, whether it's hunger, a dirty nappy or loneliness, she will be satisfied and learn that she can trust you and that you are partners.

Q: Why are newborn babies given Vitamin K?

A: Soon after birth, you will be offered Vitamin K for your baby, either by injection or in liquid drops. This vitamin is important in blood clotting and is usually given routinely. It is probably more important for preterm babies or babies who have had a difficult delivery, but discuss it with your doctor if you have any questions.

3

Settling In

‘ *I was amazed how much time it took just looking after him. All day long I just seemed to be chasing my tail and couldn't get anything done except the most basic necessities. Then I'd look at him lying there peacefully asleep, and wonder how such a tiny creature could have such an impact, running two adults around in circles.* ’

EARLY DAYS

The birth of your baby and the first few days bring an excitement which sets them apart from ordinary life. But before long you enter a new phase as you settle in at home, which involves weaving your new baby into your everyday life – an everyday life which will never be quite the same again. As well as the practical adjustments to your day which must now be organized around your baby's needs, there are emotional adjustments for everyone concerned.

When babies are born at home, settling into a rhythm after the first few days is probably easier since you are seamlessly continuing the pattern you have established since the birth. The sights, sounds and smells of home are becoming familiar to your baby, and though you have had midwives calling round, you have been on your own quite a bit and have begun setting up your own way of doing things from the beginning.

Bringing your baby home from hospital, however, means you will have an extra adjustment to make. Instead of having round-the-clock help and advice from hospital staff, you are suddenly in sole charge – a shift which can bring anxiety and doubts about whether you will manage. If you have spent more than a few days in hospital, there will also be a switch from the hospital routine to rejoining daily life at home. Your baby, too, will react to the change.

Taking plenty of time to rest and just be with your baby will help smooth the way for a gradual transition to normal everyday life.

The transition into ordinary life needs time and attention, so it's important not to try to rush too soon into the wider world, but keep your focus on yourself and your baby. Ideally, both parents being home together for a week or two after the birth will give both father and mother a chance to tune in to the baby, to learn together and build confidence with basic handling, bathing, nappy changing and so on.

'I loved people coming and having a lot of attention. It's a celebration. It can be a bit too much if people stay hours and hours, but it's nice because you can tell your story over and over, and you get advice from people and ask questions. I was on cloud nine.' FIONA

A crucial need for a new mother is rest, and her partner can help by taking responsibility for meals, shopping and housework, and looking after any other children. Along with the practical side of the father being at home, there is the importance of this time as a couple, as they cement their bonds in their new roles as parents.

Friends and relatives may be eager to come and congratulate you and admire the baby, but beware of wearing yourself out with too many visitors. You may love being the centre of so much attention, but you may also regret it later when you are exhausted with a crying baby in the middle of the night. The best visitors are those who offer to make you a cup of tea instead of expecting you to wait on them, and are sensitive about keeping a visit short. If someone calls when you are just preparing for a nap, or stays too long, do speak up and explain that you need to rest.

It may be helpful to have a relative to stay for the first few days at home. But be sure it is someone who is there to help out, not to be entertained and make more work for you. It's best if a helper sees her role as keeping every-thing running smoothly around you, leaving you and your partner plenty of time to be with your baby.

BECOMING A MOTHER

An event as large as becoming a mother is bound to affect you profoundly. Your feelings are likely to range from joy to despondency, from pride and delight in your baby to resentment at the amount of work and lack of sleep, and from excitement to frustration or boredom. It's not unusual to feel confused by experiencing seemingly opposite emotions at the same time.

'Baby blues'

A few days after giving birth or within the first week or so at home, you may be hit by a sudden plunge into feeling low. However delighted you are with your baby, you may find yourself crying forlornly for no reason you can put your finger on, or becoming irritable with those around you. Known as the 'baby blues', these feelings may be linked to the rapid hormone changes you are experiencing, and certainly tiredness is a factor. A feeling of being let down after all the anticipation of pregnancy and excitement of your baby's arrival may play a part, too. Many new mothers even feel a bit left out, as suddenly it seems everyone is interested in the baby, while she isn't very important anymore. If you do have a day where you feel down and uncontrollable tears seem to arrive from nowhere, it helps to know that the baby blues are common and short-lived.

But it's important not to put all your feelings down to baby blues as if that will explain them away, because the fact is that becoming a mother involves a huge change in your life and your view of yourself, which makes it a truly demanding time. Even changes in your life which you are happy about require adjustments and it's not always an easy process.

New role as mother

Several things are lost when you become a mother. They may be replaced by other things which are equally satisfying, or more so, but that doesn't mean you won't have some doubts or fears about letting them go.

One thing you have to let go of is your image of yourself as a child-free woman, taking on instead an image as a mother. 'Mother' means different things to different people, but you might have to reassure yourself that you can still be young, interesting, sexy and intelligent. You still need to value yourself as an individual, not just as a mother, so before long it becomes important to make sure you have time for your own interests and relaxation.

If you have given up paid work to have your baby, you might have a loss of income as well as missing satisfaction from your work. Our society rewards a job with money and the approval that comes from having met the spelled-out requirements of your work. Although you are working very hard in being a mother, society gives mothers low status. There is no one there to list your responsibilities exactly and say 'well done' when you have achieved something. So it's not surprising that confidence and self-esteem can take a dip.

You may also be missing social contacts, both through work and with friends who don't have a baby in tow. It's no longer so easy to decide on the spur of the moment to go out, and you may be too tired to be sociable when friends are free in the evenings. It is inevitable that your social life will see some changes, but the problem of isolation and loneliness can be minimized if you make the effort. Your baby is more portable in the early months before he starts solid food than he will be later, so do get out with him. Arrange to see friends midday if you need to get to bed early.

' We don't have grandparents nearby, and were quite isolated. That's where the NCT came in, introducing us to the world of other people with babies. ' HEATHER

You may lose touch with some people from your pre-child days, but your child will be a springboard to making new friends for years to come. Contact someone you met at

It may seem quite an organizational feat to get out with your baby, but it's worth the effort to avoid feeling lonely and isolated. Getting together with other mothers is a good source of companionship and support as you share your new experiences.

antenatal classes or at the baby clinic. There may be a mother-baby group in your area – ask your health visitor or local National Childbirth Trust.

Another adjustment that can be difficult to make is to adjust to 'child time'. No longer can you plan your day and stick to it, knowing when you will be working and when you have your free time. You are now on 24-hour call and you can't predict from one day to the next exactly when you will be needed. You end up trying to do several things at once and never finishing many of them. It's natural that you will sometimes find it frustrating, and feel distracted and inefficient. It doesn't help to try to impose a routine, because your baby doesn't read the clock. Gradually life will fall into more of a rhythm, but it is never fixed since your baby's needs will change as he grows and develops. Flexibility is the key and you may come to appreciate a pace of life that responds to present needs, and to feel good about your ability to keep several things in your mind at once.

Don't expect too much of yourself. Sometimes a woman who gives up work to stay home with a baby feels she must prove herself by being 'super-woman' – keeping a perfect house and producing delicious meals, while dealing single-handedly with every aspect of life with a baby. Instead, accept any help offered and take your time about becoming more organized and efficient.

Let your household standards drop so you can concentrate on the more important task of looking after yourself and your baby. As long as the essentials are done, it doesn't really matter if there is dust on the mantelpiece or there are dishes still in the sink. Most of us have certain jobs which need to be done before we can relax, while others we can happily put off until later. Work out what your personal priorities are and do the very minimum you can feel happy with.

' It's quite frightening coming home from hospital, where there were hundreds of people to tell you what to do and when. And then you get home and think, "Now what do I do?" We thought we should always be doing something with her, but gradually we learned that she'll just get on with things on her own and when she needs something she'll let us know. ' PATRICIA

Your health

All the demands of new mother-hood are easier to manage if you are feeling well physically. Don't neglect to eat well since good nutri-tion will help you recover from pregnancy and birth more quickly, as well as give you the energy you need. If you are breastfeeding, you are still providing for your baby's nutritional needs, too. You may not have time for preparing, or feel much like eating, proper meals – but stock up on healthy foods which don't require much preparation and which you can enjoy through the day.

Now is not the time to think about dieting to lose weight. Even if you are not breastfeeding, good nutrition is more important than a slim image at this point in your life and any weight loss should be gradual over several months.

Exercise is the best way for you to affect your shape, as well as your sense of well-being. Even if you feel too tired to bother, try some gentle, regular exer-cise and you'll find it increases your energy and makes you feel better.

Your need for rest cannot be overemphasized. At least once during the day, lie down and rest or sleep. If you have other small children, you could have a quiet lying-down time with them. Resist the urge to get something done whenever your baby sleeps, or while someone else looks after him – instead use the time to rest.

The postnatal check at about six weeks will give you a chance to seek advice or help on any problems, but don't wait until then, nor think it is the last word, if you have lasting pain from the birth. For some women painful stitches continue to give trouble months later, while back pain is also common. Don't think it is something you have to put up with, but seek help and if necessary be persistent and get a second opinion.

Postnatal depression

Occasionally the baby blues don't fade away quickly, but linger and grow worse. Or a mother who has been feeling well may become depressed even months after the birth. If you have signs of depression which don't pass after a week or two, any time in the first year after your baby is born, it should be taken seriously because postnatal depression can last for many months if it isn't recognized and help given. Depression doesn't necessarily mean feeling blue. It can appear as tiredness and feeling unwell, feeling hopeless, unex-plained aches and pains, difficulty sleeping, anxiety, tension and irritability, mental confusion and lack of concentration.

Postnatal depression is often a hidden illness – you may disguise it, thinking that you should be feeling happy. And other people might not recognize how badly you are feeling, because you may cheer up when you see them. It does, in fact, affect one or two out of every ten new mothers. It will pass in time, and simply knowing that can help, but real help in other ways is important.

If you think you might be depressed, talk over how you feel with your partner, family or a friend. Their extra care and understanding, as well as practical help, can give you a real boost through this period. Get plenty of rest, because depression is worse when you are tired. Talk things over with your health visitor and if your symptoms don't lift after a couple of weeks, see your doctor. You might want to take your partner or a friend with you, because it will help them understand that postnatal depression is an illness and enable them to be more supportive. Sometimes antidepressant medication can ease the symptoms of depression until things settle down and you can begin to enjoy your life and new baby more fully.

BECOMING A FATHER

Fatherhood can bring great joy, along with the sense of responsibility. Although many fathers are very close to their partners and involved in the changes of pregnancy, still you cannot be as closely aware of your baby as his mother who carries him. But at birth, seeing this new person who has sprung from you and your partner can bring wonder and both pride and humility.

TIPS FOR SETTLING IN

◆ *Get plenty of rest. Disconnect the phone when you are going for a nap.*

◆ *Do any necessary jobs early in the day while you have more energy than you will have later.*

◆ *Carrying your baby in a sling which gives good head support will soothe her and leave your hands free to get on with things.*

◆ *Keep a supply of changing things in the living room as well as the bedroom to cut down on trips around the house.*

◆ *Make lists for shopping so you can be efficient while you're out, or so someone else can do it for you.*

◆ *Use a freezer to make double batches of meals, one for now and one for later. Casseroles can be prepared earlier in the day and reheated, to avoid tension later.*

◆ *Talk to other mothers at the clinic or out shopping so you don't feel isolated – a baby is a good ice-breaker.*

◆ *Don't hover over your partner while he changes or dresses your baby. He needs to get on with it to build his feeling of competence.*

◆ *Take some time for yourself. Go shopping or exercise; a new outfit or hairstyle will give you a boost.*

Left: A father's role in baby care may range from being the occasional helper to being the primary caretaker while the mother works outside the home. Achieving the right balance is not always easy, so it is important to discuss your arrangements for childcare.
Below right: *Everything shifts when a baby comes along and new dimensions are added to your relationship with your partner. However much you enjoy your baby, though, remember that a couple still needs time to concentrate on each other.*

There may well be a down side, though. A new father faces many of the same issues as a new mother. You, too, have to deal with loss of sleep, diminished social life, possibly less available money and a new self-image as a father. If you have taken on the role of family breadwinner, you may feel under pressure from increased financial responsibility.

Some fathers find it difficult to adjust to a family of three, especially since in the early weeks much of the baby care tends to be handled by the mother, which can leave the man feeling like a spare part. You may feel jealous of the closeness between mother and baby, and miss the time spent together and the intimacy you shared with your partner before the baby arrived.

If you are involved with your baby right from the start, you are much less likely to feel left out. Even if your partner is most often in charge of the baby, you will feel competent as a parent and an integral part of the new family, when you have taken an active role from the early days. If your baby is breast-fed, you will be left out of the feeding relationship except perhaps for the occasional bottle, but your role in supporting your partner so she can breast-feed is not to be underestimated. Many fathers take delight in the peaceful sight of the mother breastfeeding their baby and benefit from the simplicity and calmness it holds.

You have your part to play in sharing baby care to allow the mother to rest and so you can build your own relationship with your baby. Bathing your baby, massage, holding and talking to him, going for a walk with your baby in a sling are all things you might enjoy.

BEING A COUPLE

Becoming parents adds a new dimension to your relationship. A new link has formed between you, in the lifelong commitment you have taken on to be parents to your child. At the same time all the work of looking after a baby and the emotional ups and downs can at times keep you apart.

Talking over how you feel so each can help support the other will bring you closer and help release pressure from any stress or strains between you. Show each other understanding and give practical help so that each of you has a break sometimes. Try to make sure you have some time together as a couple, too, so you can enjoy each other away from being parents.

Sex

While there is no right time to resume lovemaking after your baby is born, doctors generally advise not having sex in the six weeks after birth. By then some women feel ready for and interested in sex, whereas for some couples it will be much longer. Tiredness often gets in the way and a woman who has been cuddling and touching her baby all day may want some space to herself in the evening. Some couples need time to see each other as sexual partners again, instead of 'mother' and 'father'. A woman may feel uncomfortable with her body after pregnancy and she may need sensitive wooing to reassure her.

Differences in readiness for sex can cause tensions, but try to be very patient and talk over how you feel. Remember that your relationship is not just about sex – you can show you care and enjoy each other in other ways.

Soreness from stitches can delay the return to a sexual relationship. There are lots of ways besides full penetration to enjoy sex together and you could experiment and find what feels good to you. After giving birth and sometimes while breastfeeding, the vagina does not produce much lubrication, which can make sex uncomfortable. You could try using a vaginal lubricant from the chemist's and being very slow and gentle with penetration. If soreness or pain persists it may be from a problem with your stitches healing, so see your GP and ask to be referred to a gynaecologist if there is no improvement.

THE LARGER FAMILY

If you already have children, a new baby in the family will also affect them. By the age of five, a child will usually take a new arrival more or less in her stride, but a two- or three-year-old may feel displaced and very jealous. After all, when she has had you to herself all her life, it's very hard to find that suddenly she must wait for her story and has altogether much less time with you. After the initial excitement has worn off, she may well decide it's time the troublesome baby disappeared!

She may become very clingy or act in more babyish ways – wetting her bed, wanting to be fed – or show her distress in awkward behaviour which is certain to get your attention. It can be difficult to be patient when she is behaving like this, but she really needs to know that you still love her. Even with a very young child, it sometimes helps to talk about the negative feelings, and how having a baby can be a nuisance in some ways. This will help her to know that you understand and still love her even though she has these bad feelings.

Try to make times when she can have your full attention. A father can have a special role here in doing things with an older child while the mother is with the baby or rests, but it's important for a child to have time with her mother, too. You can also give her some treats or special privileges which come from being a 'big girl' so she can see there are some advantages to being an older child. Involving her in looking after the baby, giving her small jobs to do such as handing you things or smoothing lotion on the baby's feet, will help her to feel part of what's going on and that the baby isn't just yours but belongs to you all as a family.

Grandparents, too, will be welcoming the new baby. You may find a new appreciation of your parents as you identify with what they experienced when you were a baby. Grandparents may be willing helpers and can be a great source of support and advice. Ideas may have changed since they were young parents, but they also have the benefit of a greater perspective on things. So ask for advice if you want it, but be clear that you are the adult in charge of your baby and that you will make the final decisions about what is right for you and your family.

CARE SHARING

As you and your baby come to learn each other's signals and establish your own unique communication, you may feel that no one else could possibly look after your baby. In the early days and weeks after birth there may be almost an invisible umbilical cord that keeps you tied to your baby. But though your baby's attachment to you is central and unique, there is no need to exclude other people from caring for your baby.

A new baby is exciting for an older child, but it can be a mixed blessing. Sharing parents' attention may not be easy, and a small baby isn't much fun to play with. The older child needs to know she is valued, and to have you to herself sometimes.

There are several reasons why you are likely to need to arrange sharing care of your baby with someone else. It may be just for the occasional night out with your partner or for some time for yourself to follow your own interests. Or you might be planning to work away from home, either by choice or because it is financially necessary.

The first sharing of responsibility may be with your partner. It is useful to talk over your roles and agree whether childcare is mainly your area with your partner just helping out now and then, or whether you are truly planning to share the responsibility of parenthood. A pattern common to many families is for the father to take on some daily activities, such as bathtime or

' I have to focus on different things now that I'm not at work. If I found a job it would be hard to organize things for someone to look after Anna, and I'm not going to give that up. I'm lucky to have the luxury of not having to work, and I'd rather have a couple of years with her completely, with all the ups and downs. ' FIONA

playing with an older baby, while the mother undertakes all the real organization and routine care. Other couples, though, share all aspects of being parents more evenly. Then each partner can have some time to themselves, leaving the baby in competent hands.

A friend or relative may agree to look after your baby, or you may pay a babysitter or arrange reciprocal child-care with other parents. Whoever will be in charge, be sure to tell them your baby's routines and any special needs. Even with quite young babies it's best if the carer is a familiar person, but this becomes more important when your baby is a few months old and makes clear distinctions between known people and strangers.

Back to work

If you are considering going back to work you are likely to have mixed feelings. You may feel guilty about leaving your baby, concerned about good care and miss being with her. On the other hand, you may need to keep your hand in at work, need to be earning or thrive best in your job. Keep in mind that if you do enjoy your work, you will probably be more refreshed when you are with your baby – her shorter time spent with you will actually be better than spending all day together if you are frustrated and bored at home.

As long as the childcare you arrange provides consistent, loving care your baby will be fine. You and your partner may decide it suits you best for him to take on the childcare role at home while you go out to work. Or a relative may step in to look after the baby, very often a grandmother.

Other choices include a childminder, nanny or group care in a day nursery. Each of these has its advantages and disadvantages, but most important in making your choice is your own gut feeling about the quality of care – whether there is real caring for an individual child and whether you can communicate easily with the carer.

The transition will be easier if your baby already knows the carer before being left with her. Even if you plan to go back to work when your baby is several months old, it's a good idea to arrange childcare early and then spend some time with your baby and the carer before you go back to work.

If you are working, beware of overloading yourself by coming home to do most of the housework. You may feel it's not enough for your partner to take the baby for a walk while you do the cooking, but that the housework needs to be divided as well. You both need to juggle your many responsibilities, so talking over how to share everything that needs to be done will give you the best chance of meeting your needs as individuals and as a family.

QUESTIONS AND ANSWERS

Q: I feel nervous about being responsible for my baby. There are so many things I don't know and I might get something important wrong. Then people give me different advice – so who should I believe?

A: There is no end to the different views on childcare and none of them are all right or all wrong. Different things work for different parents and babies and only you can find out what suits you and your baby best. You can listen to advice, but then trust your own instincts and believe your own experience. Don't be afraid of trial and error – serious mistakes are unlikely if you use basic common sense and babies are sturdier than you may think. No parent ever gets everything right but we do the best we can, and luckily that's good enough for happy, healthy children.

Q: I'm a single parent, and finding it hard to manage everything. Do you have any suggestions?

A: Being on your own with a baby can mean extra pressures due to lack of money, loneliness and the amount of work and responsibility. Look for help from anyone willing to lend a hand and give you a break. You could contact single parents' organizations such as Gingerbread (see Appendix) to see if there is a lone parents' group in your area, or perhaps get one started. As well as the moral support of talking things over with parents in the same situation, you might exchange childcare to give you some free time. Contact the Citizens Advice Bureau for help with money matters and any benefits you may be entitled to.

Q: I expected to have a lot of time where my baby would sleep during the day or be contented, but instead he's awake most of the day and has to be carried or held all the time. Isn't this unusual?

A: It's hard when the reality of life with your baby doesn't match your expectations. Parents who have a firm idea of what to expect, sometimes based on what their first baby or another baby they've known was like, actually find it harder to cope than those who just take it as it comes. Every baby is different and while some have a placid temperament others are more demanding and need to be held and comforted more. The amount of sleep a young baby needs varies a lot, too. Try not to think about an average baby, or an ideal baby, but focus on your baby as an individual and what he needs.

Q: If I leave my baby with my mother, could she get attached to her instead of me?

A: A baby doesn't have to make just one bond, but can be attached to two or more people. Often the closest bond is to the mother, but the baby can also be attached to others who will do when the mother isn't there. It's nice if your baby does become attached to your mother, because that means she is being well cared for, but as long as you are there for important times like bedtime and your daughter knows she can trust your love, your mother won't be taking your place in her eyes.

4

Feeding Your Baby

' *It never entered my mind to use a bottle. Breastfeeding is so much easier – it's always there, ready, and I think it's better. Some of my friends don't really like to do it, and breastfeed because they think they should. But I think it's nicer. It's natural, and she seems to like it.* '

MORE THAN JUST NOURISHMENT

Far more than just providing nourishment for growing and developing, feeding your baby is also a time of special closeness. For your baby, it brings the bliss of a satisfied stomach, being held in your arms and able to watch your face and play with you. For you it is a peaceful lull with the pleasure of your baby snuggled against you, hearing her first eager and then contented swallows and seeing her break off to smile at you or drift into sleep.

Breastmilk is definitely the ideal food for babies, who will benefit from being given nothing else for the first four to six months of life. It offers several advantages over formula milk, both for your baby's health and for you. If you choose to bottlefeed, or end up using a bottle because of feeding problems, your baby will still thrive and the closeness of feeding times can still be central for both you and your baby.

BREASTFEEDING

Breastmilk is the perfect food designed by nature to suit human babies and it is such a complex and changing substance that even the best formula milks cannot copy it exactly.

Advantages

Ideal food: It contains not only the ideal amounts and types of protein, fats, sugars, vitamins and minerals, but also protective factors, certain hormones and enzymes which help to make it digestible for your baby. Not all the substances in breastmilk are fully understood and more are discovered all the time, so it is impossible to duplicate.

Breastmilk changes as your baby grows so that it meets your baby's changing needs. The very first milk, colostrum, is ideal for a newborn as it is rich in antibodies, fat and protein, and helps to clear the baby's bowel and give it a protective lining. Breastmilk itself varies when produced for a premature baby, a young baby or an older baby. It also changes within a feed, so that the first milk satisfies your baby's thirst, followed by richer milk to satisfy hunger. This gives your baby more control over how much nourishment she will take, and helps to prevent her becoming overweight, as a baby and in later life.

Protection from illness: Breastfed babies are far less likely to suffer from gastroenteritis and diarrhoea, partly because breastmilk is always sterile and free from bacteria and partly because it contains substances which coat the intestinal wall and prevent the absorption of micro-organisms.

Infectious illnesses are also much less likely because breastfed babies have better immunity in the first few months. During pregnancy your baby was protected by your antibodies, and after several weeks she will gradually begin to make her own. Breastfeeding fills the gap for a young baby as the antibodies and white blood cells which fight infection are passed on in the milk.

Avoiding allergies: Allergies such as eczema, asthma and hay fever are less likely in a breastfed baby and when they do arise they tend to appear later and be less severe. This effect is again linked to the protective coating of the gut and to avoiding substances such as cow's milk proteins which may trigger allergies. Particularly if there are allergies in your family, exclusive breastfeeding for the first six months or more offers your baby the best protection against developing allergies.

'The only problems I had breastfeeding were that I was quite sore and had to wear shields for the first few weeks, and that I had far too much milk. I literally had to get up in the night and change the bed for weeks, and when I fed on one side I had to hold a towel to the other breast to catch the flow.' PATRICIA

Economy: Breastmilk is free, with no need to buy feeding and sterilizing equipment and formula milk, representing quite a saving over a few months.

Convenience: Breastmilk is always ready – sterile and at exactly the right temperature – without washing and sterilizing, mixing and heating. It's far easier to take your baby anywhere, and night feeds are much less tiring because you can feed your baby in bed so you hardly need to wake.

Good for you: Breastfeeding releases hormones which help your uterus shrink back to normal more quickly. Although you need to eat well and may feel quite hungry while breastfeeding, many breastfeeding mothers find they lose weight more easily from the amount of calories burnt up in producing milk. Breastfeeding may also give you some protection against cancer of the breast, ovaries and cervix in later life.

Satisfying: Many mothers love the sensation of feeding their babies and the feeling that they are still providing for their baby as they did before birth. The

Breastfeeding is convenient, which is a great boon to busy parents. There is no work preparing feeds, nothing to carry on outings, and the milk is always ready, sterile, and the right temperature – even for feeding your baby on the beach, like this mother.

51

skin-to-skin contact provides a special intimacy which may help with bonding, while the hormone which triggers milk production, prolactin, also promotes your motherly feelings and a sense of peace and relaxation.

Your baby likes to nurse not just for food, but also for the comfort and pleasure it gives her. She couldn't be allowed to bottlefeed just for comfort, because of the risk of becoming obese from overfeeding, but even when the breast is empty she can still continue to nurse for the comfort and satisfaction it provides.

How milk is made

During pregnancy your hormones stimulate development of the milk-producing cells in your breasts, so that by late pregnancy they begin to produce small amounts of colostrum. After the birth a sudden rise in the hormone, prolactin, brings about the first milk production, but from then on it is breastfeeding your baby which causes the milk to continue being produced. It is in fact a perfect supply-and-demand system – the more your baby feeds, the more milk is made, so there will always be the right amount for your baby's needs.

When your baby sucks on the breast, a message is sent from the nerves in your nipple to the pituitary gland in your brain – in effect telling your system that the baby needs milk and how much. The pituitary gland responds by releasing two hormones – prolactin which causes the milk to be produced and oxytocin which helps release the milk in the breast for your baby.

To express milk, support your breast with one hand while with the other hand you place your thumb and fingers on opposite sides, well behind the nipple at the edge of the areola. First press back toward your chest wall, then bring your thumb and fingers together, and roll forward slightly. Continue this motion, and be patient as it may take a while to get it right. A warm flannel placed on the breast before expressing may help the milk to flow. Rotate the position of your hand to empty different areas of the breast.

The milk is produced in cells called alveoli, each of which is surrounded by muscle cells which can contract to squeeze the alveoli and send the milk down ducts toward the nipple. Before reaching the nipple, the ducts widen to become reservoirs for milk just behind the nipple (see page 55).

' When I went back to work I hired a machine pump to express milk to leave for Jessamine, and it worked quite well though I sometimes felt like a cow on a milking machine. She always refused to take a bottle from me, when she knew she could have the breast, but she would accept a bottle from my husband. ' HEATHER

Your baby doesn't actually suck on the nipple, but takes it fairly far back in her mouth as an anchor and keeps it there with a bit of suction, as her jaws open and close on the area around the nipple, the areola. This forces the milk stored in the reservoirs out through the openings in the nipple and your baby receives this first 'foremilk' of the feed, which has less fat and calories than the later milk but is more thirst-quenching.

In response to her sucking, the oxytocin released causes the muscles around the alveoli to contract, sending the richer milk streaming down from where it is produced right to your baby. This is called the 'letdown' reflex, and you may feel it as a tingling far back in the breast. Once the letdown has occurred your baby doesn't have to suck very much, as the hindmilk comes in a steady trickle or even a spurting stream, and she needs only a bit of suction to anchor the nipple in her mouth while she swallows the milk.

Getting started

Ideally the first feed takes place sometime in the first hour or so after birth, while your baby is alert. A good start in this period teaches both you and your baby and helps set a pattern that can continue through all your feeding experience. Some babies, though, are not interested in sucking very soon after birth, or you may be unable to put the baby to the breast right away if you have had an anaesthetic or your baby needs special care. In that case, taking time at the earliest opportunity to have the first feed will get things started.

A calm atmosphere and some privacy are important to help you and your baby relax and learn together. An experienced midwife will guide you if you feel uncertain. Though later you may find it easy and restful to feed your baby lying down, it is easier for the first feed to be sitting up. You can put a pillow on your lap to support your arm holding your baby, so you don't have to lean forward and strain your back.

Your baby's position is as important as yours. Hold him with his neck in the crook of your elbow and your forearm supporting his body. His back should be straight, with his head slightly higher than his body, and he should be free to turn his head or pull it back. Don't place him tummy up, because he would then have to turn his head to the side to feed – just try swallowing with your head turned. Instead, turn his whole body to face you, belly against your belly.

Never try to put a crying baby or baby with a closed mouth to the breast, but wait until he is calm and has his mouth wide open. If you put him to the breast before his mouth is opened he will not latch on properly and it will cause sore nipples. A newborn baby has a strong rooting reflex which makes him turn his head and open his mouth when touched lightly on the cheek. Touch him lightly with a finger on the side nearest the nipple to help him find it (see opposite page). Sometimes, expressing a drop of colostrum will trigger his interest because he will notice its sweet smell.

When your baby's mouth is open, bring him to the breast. Don't try to bring the breast to him – it would cause you to stoop and cause back problems and he won't latch on as well. And don't try to push his head towards you or have a helper hold the back of his head, because he will instinctively push his head back into the touch instead of towards the breast. Instead simply bring your arm closer to bring him to the breast, aiming so that his lower lip is far down on the areola, the coloured part around the nipple. Another way to think of it is aiming him so the nipple points at the roof of his mouth. He will then latch on and begin to suck.

You may feel surprised at the sensation of his first sucking, which may be quite strong. It is his instinct to suck, but very quick learning is involved, too. He learns that colostrum, and then milk, comes from the sucking. Within a very short time he learns that when he is hungry and put in the position for a feed, he can stop crying and get on with finding the nipple.

How often?

Feed your baby whenever she seems to want feeding. Some new babies want to be at the breast for much of the time in the first few days, and all this stimulation may help your milk come in more quickly. Other babies are rather sleepy and those who still have some drugs in their system from the birth may not have a strong urge to suck. Take your cue from your baby, with a good guideline being to put her to the breast whenever she wakes during the first few days.

After the milk comes in and the supply begins to settle down to match your baby's needs she will generally have longer gaps between feeds. Breastmilk is easily digested so her stomach will normally be empty two to three hours after a feed, but she may want a feed only 15 minutes after the last. Perhaps she is thirsty now and wants just the foremilk this time. Or it may be that she is in a growth spurt and her appetite has increased. Putting her to the breast again will satisfy her for now, and a day or two of frequent feeds will increase your milk supply so her requirements will be met with fewer, larger feeds again.

So in the beginning, as later on, a breastfed baby will let you know how often she needs a feed and you can trust her messages. If in doubt, you can always offer the breast. She won't be interested or will cut it short if it's not really what she needs.

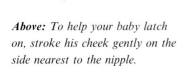

Above: To help your baby latch on, stroke his cheek gently on the side nearest to the nipple.
Right: Settle yourself comfortably with your back straight to breastfeed. It helps to place a cushion under a very young baby.

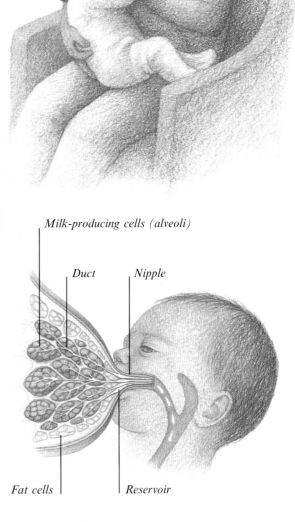

Above: To release the nipple mid-feed, insert the tip of your finger gently into the corner of your baby's mouth.
Right: In response to your baby sucking, milk travels from the milk-producing cells (alveoli) down the ducts to the nipple.

Milk-producing cells (alveoli)

Duct *Nipple*

Fat cells *Reservoir*

How long?

There is no need to limit the amount of time at the breast. Since your baby is not actually sucking on the nipple, but just holding it back in her mouth, it will not become sore from the time she spends on the breast. So let her stay as long as she likes and she will stop when she is finished.

It is true that you may have some soreness in the first few days before the nipple skin toughens up. It usually feels worst when the baby first latches on and is then relieved after the letdown occurs. For many women this is thankfully just a short-lived process that must be got through and it is not prevented by limiting the time at each breast to just a few minutes. In fact, if your baby sucks as long as she likes you are likely to get through the period of soreness more quickly, rather than delaying the toughening-up process.

One reason it is important not to remove your baby from the breast before she is ready is that the letdown of the richer hindmilk may not happen until several minutes into the feed. If you change breasts or stop feeding before the letdown occurs, your baby will not receive the full nourishment of the feed. So let her have as much as she likes from one side. Then you can offer her the other breast, in case she wants a drink of the more refreshing foremilk to finish off the feed.

If she still seems hungry after the second breast, you can change her back to the first again, as there will have been a further letdown of milk and more will now be available.

TIPS FOR BREASTFEEDING

◆ *If milk drips from the other breast while your baby feeds, pressing firmly against the nipple with your hand may stop the flow.*

◆ *Tops which pull up easily make feeding in public discreet.*

◆ *Most women prefer nursing bras which fully open from the front, rather than just dropping a flap, and they are less likely to cause a blocked duct by pressing unevenly on the breast.*

◆ *Drugs may be passed on through your milk, so be sure your doctor knows you are breastfeeding and ask the pharmacist about any over-the-counter medicines.*

◆ *Your baby does not need extra water to drink, even in hot weather. Just feed more often.*

◆ *Some babies react to certain foods in your diet, with a crying colicky spell. You can check by leaving out a food you suspect and then trying it again after a couple of weeks.*

◆ *Beware of switching to bottlefeeding because of being tired. You might find yourself just as tired, but with even more work to do in preparing bottles. Rest is the key for all new mothers, breastfeeding or not.*

It is not necessary to feed from both breasts at each feed. If your baby is satisfied with just one breast, start with the more full breast next time so that both breasts are emptied fairly regularly and so receive stimulation to keep producing milk.

If you do need to interrupt a feed for any reason, don't just pull your baby off the breast, which could make your nipples sore. Break the suction first by pulling down gently on her chin, or by slipping a finger inside the corner of her mouth (see page 55).

Enough milk

As long as you feed your baby whenever he is hungry there should be no problem in producing enough milk. Size and shape of breasts make no difference to the ability to produce milk, since breast size is determined by layers of fat around the milk-producing cells, and even the smallest breasts can make just as much milk.

Sometimes women worry that their milk is of poor quality, because it looks thinner and bluish-white after the first few days. That is how breastmilk looks after it gradually changes from the creamier-looking colostrum and it is exactly right. Another cause for worry can be when the breasts do not feel full. When your milk first comes in the breasts are usually very full and look voluptuous, but after a few weeks as the production settles down to match the baby's needs the breasts may remain soft and never feel full, even though in fact they are producing much more milk than in the early days.

If your baby seems fretful and not satisfied after a feed, don't be tempted to top him up with a bottle. Because formula milk is slower to digest than breastmilk he won't be interested in the breast for a longer time and your breasts won't get the stimulation they need to make more milk. Also, the idea that a bottle at night will give you a chance to rest and make more milk is false. Night feeds are especially important, as they may boost your milk supply even more than daytime ones. Remember that it's a supply-and-demand system, and whatever milk your baby takes from a bottle is that much less your breasts will make.

Instead, keep switching your baby back to the other breast when he has finished with one. He will then receive more milk and your breasts will be getting the message about producing more. You may find that he needs feeding again fairly soon, but if you keep up frequent feeds for a day or two your supply will soon catch up.

Rest and good food

Getting enough rest is important for good milk production. Do not rush around too much and try to have a nap or at least put your feet up each afternoon. Luckily the breastfeeding hormones help you relax and sleep more soundly at night.

BREASTFEEDING – POSSIBLE PROBLEMS

You may have few or none of the problems listed below, but some difficulties are common in the early weeks. Many can be overcome with perseverance and expert help from your midwife, health visitor or breastfeeding counsellor. Fortunately, after early adjustments, breastfeeding usually settles down to become a simple pleasure.

PROBLEM	CAUSE	WHAT TO DO
Engorgement	Breasts overfull as milk comes in, or from missing feeds.	Feed baby often to keep up with supply; warm bathing before a feed softens breasts and helps baby latch on; express a little milk to help baby grasp nipple; cold compresses after feed relieve swelling.
Afterpains	Hormones released in feeding cause uterus to contract; may be painful in early days, especially with second or later babies.	Try to relax and breathe deeply; the rhythmic contractions are getting your uterus back to normal quickly; beware of painkillers which will be passed on in your milk.
Sore nipples	Pain at beginning of feed caused by suction.	This is a normal feeling and will soon lessen or stop.
	Pain throughout feed; baby not latched on properly.	Faulty breastfeeding position; ask midwife or feeding counsellor to see if baby is latched on correctly.
	Sensitivity from soap, creams or sprays.	Avoid products on nipples; plain water is enough; dry cornflour is soothing.
	Nipples wet.	Avoid soggy breast pads, especially when plastic-lined; expose to air as much as possible.
Cracked nipple	May develop from sore nipple, especially if baby is not latching on properly.	If very painful to feed, rest breast for one or two feeds, expressing milk and feeding from other side; nipple shields can give protection.

PROBLEM	CAUSE	WHAT TO DO
Inverted or flat nipple	Your natural shape may mean the nipple is difficult for the baby to grasp.	If possible, contact a breastfeeding counsellor during pregnancy, when stretching exercises may bring the nipple forward; in early feeds a rubber shield can help until the baby's sucking draws the nipple forward.
Tender lump in breast; feels red and hot	Blocked duct.	Continue to feed often; put a damp hot flannel on the sore place often and before feeds; massage sore breast in a hot bath before feed; change baby's position during feeds to be sure all areas are emptied; be sure bra or clothing isn't pressing on breast.
As for blocked duct, but also flu-like signs	Mastitis, an infection in the breast; may be from germ entering nipple crack, or milk left in overfull breasts.	See your doctor, who may prescribe antibiotics; continue to breastfeed unless specifically advised not to; express milk if not feeding and follow other advice as for blocked duct.
Baby not gaining weight	Baby may be ill.	Have doctor examine baby.
	No letdown of milk.	Relax for feeds; put a warm flannel on breasts before feed; don't limit the time at each breast; check baby is latched on.
	Use of dummy or bottles decreases sucking at breast.	Cut out; increase sucking at the breast instead.
	Underfeeding	Boost milk supply with frequent feeds, rest and good diet; give complementary bottlefeeds only if there is no sign of improvement.

BOTTLEFEEDING

There are many reasons why you may decide to bottlefeed your baby and you can expect your baby to thrive on the carefully produced formula milk available. You may decide from the outset that you want to feed with a bottle, or you may start out breastfeeding and then switch. There are advantages for your baby in receiving the first food from the breast, the colostrum, because it helps provide immune protection and guards against digestive problems. So you might want to start at the breast in any case. If all goes smoothly and you then want to stay with breastfeeding, you can; if you do switch to bottles quite soon your baby has still had a good start which formula milk can't quite provide.

Many mothers switch to bottles before they really want to because of difficulties with breastfeeding and may then feel disappointed, frustrated or angry. It is true that although there is much said about the benefits of breastfeeding, sometimes help with problems can be thin on the ground. If you are having problems and want to continue breastfeeding, you could try contacting a breastfeeding counsellor (see Appendix) who will have a lot of experience from mothers' points of view and can give you help and advice.

It is also true, though, that although it may be possible to overcome most breastfeeding problems, there are situations where it may not be worth the effort and worry it can cause you. For you to be happy, relaxed, comfortable and confident about feeding your baby is probably the most important thing. Only you can know how the balance falls for you and your baby, and you can give yourself credit for making the best decision for your circumstances.

Why bottlefeed?

Sharing feeding: With bottlefeeding the baby's father can give feeds, as well as enjoying his baby in other ways. Other family members, too, can give an occasional bottle. The mother is less tied and can be more flexible about arranging time for her own activities if she knows her baby can be fed by someone else in her absence.

Going out to work: If you are planning to go back to work and will need someone else to feed your baby, you may feel it will be easier to start out with bottles. Or you might decide to start your baby on the breast, but perhaps introduce an occasional bottle so she will be used to taking milk from the bottle in preparation for your return to work.

' In the early weeks when Carol was breastfeeding I sometimes felt quite jealous that there was nothing I could do, and I couldn't help at night when she was tired. But after eight or ten weeks we sometimes gave him a bottle, and I found it nice and reassuring to be able to feed him. ' PETER

Social or family pressures: In some families bottlefeeding is the norm, so you might feel self-conscious about breastfeeding. Or perhaps your husband doesn't want you to breastfeed. Some women worry

A feed is above all a time of closeness and sharing. Your baby might like you to talk or hum to her. Some hungry babies feed steadily, while others may prefer to break off for a smile and a little 'chat' before going back to their milk.

about feeding their baby in public when they are out. With these sorts of pressure, you might feel more comfortable and happy feeding with a bottle.

Physical reasons: There may be a physical condition in the mother such as an illness, necessary drugs which would appear in breastmilk, or inverted nipples or other problems which make feeding difficult and don't improve over time. Certain problems in the baby such as cleft palate can also make breastfeeding difficult or impossible.

Emotional reasons: Some women simply don't like the idea of breastfeeding, or feel uncomfortable with the emotional side of having a baby so closely dependent, attached and intimate in feeding. In this case there is no point in breastfeeding and feeling unhappy, when she could feel warm and loving to her baby by giving a bottle feed.

Choosing a formula

Formula milk is usually derived from cow's milk, although some are based on soya protein. There are many differences between cow's milk and human milk, so the milk is 'humanized' to make it as close as possible to breastmilk in the amount of protein, fats, carbohydrates, vitamins and minerals. Because a calf grows much more quickly than a baby, cow's milk contains three times as much protein so it is diluted in the manufacture of infant formula. The protein is also a different type, casein, which is bulky and hard for a baby to digest. Processing the cow's milk proteins makes them more digestible but the milk still takes longer for a baby to digest, which is why a bottlefed baby tends to have about four hours between feeds instead of two or three for a breastfed baby.

Formula milk will also have added sugars to match the amount of milk sugar in breastmilk and minerals are removed so there will not be a strain on the baby's kidneys. Skimmed milk and unsaturated vegetable oils are also added to approximate the types of fat in breastmilk.

Although many different brands and types of formula are available, any of the humanized milks will be suitable and it is best to choose one type and stick with it, rather than changing back and forth. If you think there may be a problem with the formula, discuss it with your health visitor or doctor.

Some babies are allergic to cow's milk protein in formula, and may need to have a soya-based formula. But your baby is just as likely to be allergic to soya proteins, so don't change without consulting your doctor.

Equipment

You will need six to eight bottles, unbreakable with wide necks for easy cleaning, and about a dozen teats. You might want to look out for teats which are shaped to copy the sucking action of breastfeeding. Sometimes called 'orthodontic' teats, these may be better for the baby's developing jaw and can make it easier if you want to combine breast- and bottlefeeding.

You will also need sterilizing equipment, including a sterilizing bath and tablets, a bottle brush, measuring jug, long-handled spoon and a knife.

Sterilizing

Everything you use in preparing formula and feeding your baby for at least the first four months must be sterilized, because milk is a perfect place for bacteria to grow and your baby could easily become ill if all germs are not destroyed.

First wash bottles carefully in warm soapy water, cleaning the inside with a brush to remove all traces of formula. Rub the inside of teats with salt and rinse carefully. When items are clean, they can then be sterilized.

The most common way to sterilize equipment is in a large unit filled with water in which you dissolve a sterilizing tablet or add concentrated sterilizing fluid. Follow the manufacturer's directions as to how long items must be left in the solution. Everything must be fully submerged, so make sure there are no air bubbles in bottles or teats. Once they have been in the solution for the correct time there is no need to rinse equipment before use, though you may prefer to rinse with boiled water to remove the strong chlorine smell.

Alternatively, you can sterilize bottles and the measuring jug in a normal dishwater cycle, using tablets to sterilize teats, or with a special sterilizing unit in a microwave. Steam sterilizers (electric units for sealed sterilizing of equipment) are also available. Follow manufacturer's instructions for use.

TIPS FOR BOTTLEFEEDING

◆ *If your breasts become engorged when your milk comes in, a good supporting bra will help with discomfort which lasts a day or two. If necessary your doctor can prescribe a drug to stop you producing milk.*

◆ *Cooled boiled water can be offered between feeds if your baby is thirsty. Do not use sweetened herbal or fruity drinks which your baby does not need and which can decay baby teeth.*

◆ *Don't leave your baby with a propped-up bottle. Aside from the danger of choking, your baby needs you.*

◆ *Once milk is warmed, feed your baby immediately so there is no time for any bacteria to build up.*

◆ *Never use a thermos flask to keep milk warm – this is a perfect breeding ground for germs. If you are going out, you could keep warm boiled water in a flask, then add it to the milk powder in a sterilized bottle when required.*

◆ *Changing sides partway through a feed gives your arms a rest, and gives your baby a new view of the world.*

Making up feeds

It will save time if you make up at one time all the feeds you are likely to need for a day. First wash your hands carefully. Boil the water you will use for the feeds and then allow to cool to lukewarm before pouring it into the sterile jug. Check the formula tin to work out how much you need to mix up, according to your baby's age and weight. It's a good idea to put a little more than you expect your baby to want into each bottle, so that if she is extra hungry you don't have to start on another bottle as well, since any then left over must be thrown away.

Fill the required number of scoops with powder, levelling with the sterile knife before adding the powder to the water in the jug. It is crucial to use *level* scoops, and never to add more scoops than recommended, because milk which is too strong strains your baby's kidneys and can make her thirsty.

Stir well with the sterilized spoon until the powder is dissolved, then pour the milk into the sterile bottles. Place the teats upside down into the bottles, and secure with the lids. Then immediately put the filled bottles into the refrigerator, where they must be kept until ready for use.

If you use liquid formula, wash the lid well before opening, and use a sterile can opener and equipment as above.

When to feed your baby

Feed your baby whenever she is hungry. If you have decided to bottlefeed right from the beginning, your baby's first feed may be sugared water. She may not be very hungry in the first day or two, but you can feed her when she cries for milk. Soon she will probably settle into roughly four-hour intervals between feeds. There will be times, though, when she sleeps longer or when she wants more feeds in a day and you can take your lead from her.

Giving a bottlefeed

Settle yourself comfortably with your baby. Be sure you are sitting with your back straight to avoid strain and fatigue. This is a time for you both to enjoy, so give her all your attention. Stroke her cheek nearest you so she will turn to find the teat and be ready to suck. Then gently slide the teat into her mouth. Hold the bottle tilted so that the teat is completely filled with milk, so it flows well and she won't be swallowing air.

Feeding is a sociable time, so look at your baby, talk to her or hum or sing to her. She might want to take a break from her feed and then come back to it, so let her set the pace.

Halfway through the feed, especially if your baby pauses, it's a good idea to burp your baby to bring up any air she might have swallowed so she can comfortably take her full feed. You can put a cloth over your shoulder and hold her upright against your shoulder, gently stroking or patting her back, lay her across your lap tummy down and pat her back or support her upright on your lap in a sitting position while you rub or pat her back (see page 25).

Let your baby decide when she has had enough. Don't coax her to finish a bottle, which may result in her being overfull so she brings the milk back or in becoming overweight. Just discard any milk left in the bottle at the end of a feed. If she finishes a bottle and wants more, you can go on to another bottle and then discard any remaining in the second bottle. Increase the amount in the bottles if she finishes feeds and is fretful or hungry again after only a couple of hours.

Twins can be fully breastfed, either feeding both at once or one after the other. The position shown here works well, or one baby can lie across the mother's front with the other at her side. The extra sucking signals the breasts to make enough milk for two babies.

QUESTIONS AND ANSWERS

Q: I will be going back to work when my baby is a few weeks old, but am reluctant to give up breastfeeding altogether. Is it possible to do both?

A: Yes, you can combine breast and bottlefeeding. It's not a good idea combining the two right at the beginning when breastfeeding is being established, but after you begin work your milk supply will soon adjust to how much your baby takes if you feed your baby just in the morning and evening. Do introduce a bottle in time to get your baby used to taking milk from a teat.

Q: Is it possible to breastfeed twins?

A: Twins can be fully breastfed, although it would be very time-consuming to feed completely on demand as you would with one baby. Mothers of twins often feed both babies at one time, sitting up with a baby at each breast lying alongside her with their feet toward her back (see opposite page). Another approach is to feed one baby when it wakes, then wake and feed the other so it is still basically one feeding session. A breastfeeding mother of twins needs lots of practical help so she can rest, and an excellent diet.

Q: My baby brings back lots of milk. Is he getting enough nourishment?

A: See your doctor to rule out possible problems, but the answer will probably be that it is nothing to worry about. The valve at the entrance to the stomach is very loose in young babies and milk can come out nearly as easily as it goes in. Some babies do bring milk back very freely and although it is messy it does no harm. As long as you feed your baby when he is hungry, and he is contented, alert and sociable you can be confident he is getting enough milk. If you are bottlefeeding, be careful not to coax him into taking too much which can trigger the overflow. Keep plenty of cloths handy for mopping up and it might help to prop your baby up at an angle for a while after feeds. He will outgrow it eventually.

Q: Is it necessary to warm my baby's bottle?

A: Though your baby's feed does not have to be warm, most babies seem to prefer warm milk. You can use a purpose-made bottle warmer, or simply stand the bottle in a basin of hot water or hold it under the hot tap. Using a microwave is not recommended because the milk can be very hot while the bottle still feels cool, and there can be uneven hot spots in the milk. If you do use a microwave, shake the bottle well to mix the milk and disperse heat. However you heat a bottle, always check the temperature of the milk before giving it to your baby. Let a few drops fall on the inside of your wrist to check that it is comfortably body temperature and not hot.

Q: How should I check the flow of milk from the teat?

A: With the bottle tipped up there should be a steady drip from the teat. If it comes in a stream the hole is too big and may cause your baby to splutter and choke. If it doesn't drip at all, or only slowly, the hole is too small and will make your baby work too hard to feed. You can enlarge the hole with a needle heated to red-hot, which will melt the rubber.

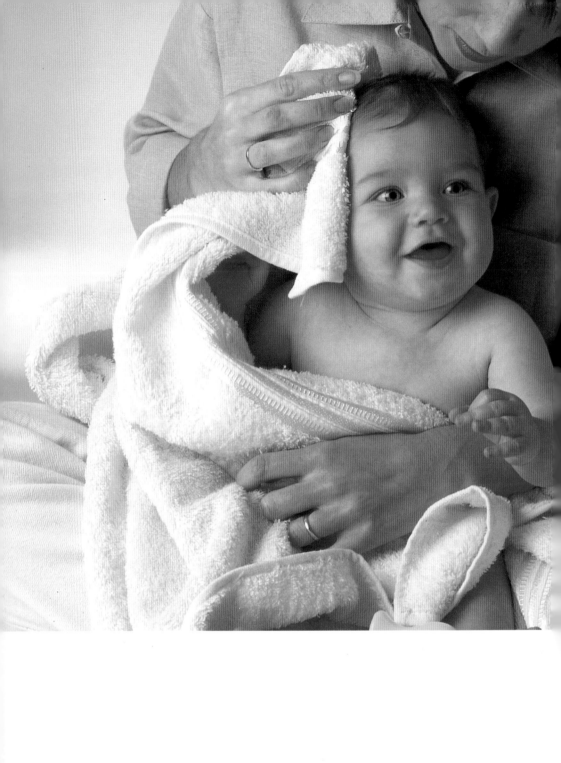

5

Clean and Comfortable

' When I was organizing baby clothes before Robert was born my husband joked that I just wanted to play dolls. It is fun dressing him up to show him off, but mostly it's a matter of lots of changes because he's dribbled milk or leaked around his nappy. '

CHANGING NEEDS

From the newborn baby who spends most of his day sleeping in a basket or cradled in your arms, to the crawling explorer who goes everywhere, reaches into everything and puts whatever he finds straight into his mouth, is only a matter of a few months' time. Keeping him clean and comfortably dressed will be a different task as he grows, but is always an important part of the daily routine for you and your baby.

NAPPIES

Once your baby is taking full milk feeds after the first couple of days, you can expect from about six to 12 wet nappies per day. As your baby grows he will stay dry for longer periods, because the bladder can hold more before it automatically empties.

When do nappies need changing?

A baby's urine is pale, not strong, and sterile, and normally it does no harm to leave him wet for a while as long as the nappy is not also soiled. Some babies do seem to feel uncomfortable and object to being wet, so if your baby complains do change him.

Dirty nappies need changing promptly, because as well as being uncomfortable the stool is full of bacteria which act on urine to form ammonia – this irritates tender skin and causes nappy rash. Your baby's first bowel movement produces meconium, a dark sticky tar-like substance which has been in the bowel before birth. Over the next few days the stools gradually change to those of a milk-fed baby.

If your baby is breastfed, his stools will be from almost liquid to soft and pasty, and vary in colour from the typical mustard yellow to greenish. Because breastmilk is almost completely absorbed in your baby's digestion, he may have a bowel movement only every few days. As long as the stool is soft when it appears, this is normal and is not a case of constipation. At the other end of the scale, it is also normal for a breastfed baby to have several bowel movements a day, usually as a reflex action of the gut triggered by a feed. Diarrhoea caused by gastroenteritis is pretty rare in breastfed babies, so you need be concerned about frequent motions only if the stool is watery and there are other signs of illness.

A bottlefed baby's stools will probably be more formed and brownish in colour, because formula milk stays longer in the gut. There should be at least one bowel movement per day. It is possible for a bottlefed baby to become constipated, but again judge this more by whether the stool is hard than by complete regularity of motions. If you think your baby may

'*It helps if you own a laundry! We were astonished at how much laundry one tiny baby can generate. We have found that the washing machine is on at least twice a day.*'
ANDREW

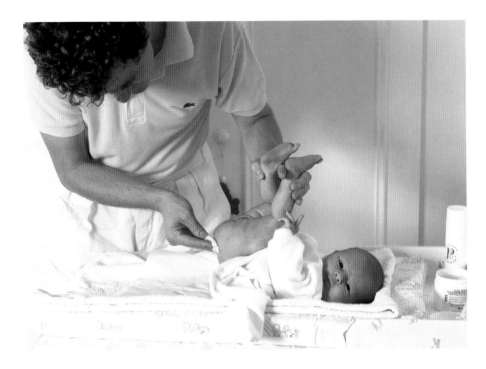

be constipated, be sure you are not adding too much milk powder to bottles and offer cooled boiled water for drinks between feeds. If it persists, see your doctor or health visitor to discuss any further steps you might take.

Plain water on a cotton wool ball is enough to clean your baby if her nappy is only wet. Lotion may make the job easier when she is soiled. Protective nappy cream helps if your baby's skin is very sensitive, but avoid powders.

When a young baby wakes crying with hunger, changing him before feeding will result in frantic crying and difficulty settling to a calm feed. He will probably need changing afterwards anyway, so you can wait to change him after the feed. During the night some parents like to change a baby mid-feed, so he can doze off in the second half of the feed and won't be roused by changing afterwards. An older baby will have learned that once you are there his feed won't be far behind, and can be patient during changing first – then he can have his feed in comfort.

What kind of nappies?

Choosing nappies means weighing up the pros and cons which are most important to you and which are most appropriate to your way of life. It's a good occasion for gathering experiences and recommendations of other mothers. If you're not sure, before lashing out on the initial expenses of terries or reusable nappies, why not start with disposables which are very easy for a new baby and then make up your mind when you are a bit more settled.

Disposables are also very easy when travelling, so you might like to use them then, whatever you normally use at home.

Terries: The traditional terry nappy has some advantages, including price. Although they are an initial expense, you don't have to keep buying nappies and they can be handed down to a later baby. When folded in one of a variety of styles, they can fit your baby well. Some parents like the fact that they are a natural fabric and feel they are more comfortable for a baby to wear. You might also appreciate that they are much kinder to the environment than disposables because trees aren't used in their manufacture and they don't cause waste disposal problems.

On the minus side, they are more fiddly to use than disposables and some reusables and they are bulky for a baby to wear. Quite a bit of work is involved in sterilizing, washing and folding (and the washing and cleaning chemicals also take their toll environmentally).

Also available are shaped terry nappies, with a thick central absorbent layer and thinner terry on the sides. These may make a more comfortable fit for your baby but take longer to dry.

If you decide on terry nappies you will need at least 24 to allow for washing and drying time. You will also need waterproof pants and safety pins with locking heads. Paper nappy liners are softer for your baby and make changing easier, while one-way liners draw moisture away from your baby's skin to keep him drier. (See opposite page for folding a terry nappy.)

Reusables: A range of washable, reusable nappies is available to bridge some of the gaps between traditional fabric nappies and disposables. They are cheaper and better for the environment than disposables and can last more than one baby. Compared to terries, they are easier to use, more attractive and offer a more snugly adjustable fit. Machine washable, they can be tumble dried but take around 24 hours to dry naturally.

Various styles are available, including all-in-one waterproof pants with cloth lining and absorbent padding, usually with elasticated legs and adjustable Velcro waist fasteners. Two-piece varieties include similar shaped cloth nappies with separate outer waterproof pants, or waterproof pants or wraps with pockets for absorbent pads to be inserted inside.

Disposables: Disposable nappies certainly win for convenience, except for regularly shopping for fairly bulky packages. Varieties are available for all sizes of baby, from low birthweight to toddler's overnight size. Most offer a good adjustable fit with reusable waist tapes and elasticated legs, a one-way lining to keep baby's skin dry, and good absorbency. Manufacturers usually produce different varieties for girls and boys.

Disposables are easy to use and require no washing. Care must be taken in disposing of soiled nappies, preferably with stools flushed down the toilet (easier if you have used a nappy liner in the disposable) before placing the nappy in a plastic bag, to be sealed before putting in the wastebin.

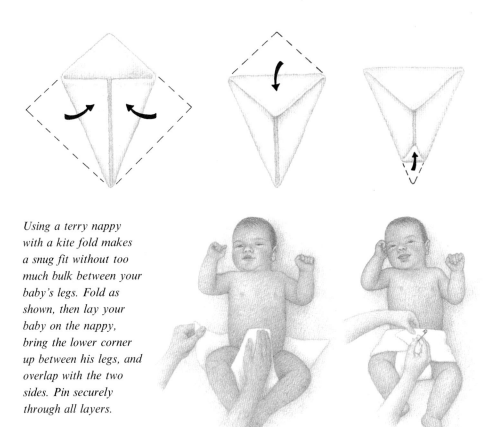

Using a terry nappy with a kite fold makes a snug fit without too much bulk between your baby's legs. Fold as shown, then lay your baby on the nappy, bring the lower corner up between his legs, and overlap with the two sides. Pin securely through all layers.

TIPS FOR NAPPY CHANGING

◆ *Fifteen minutes without a nappy promotes healthy skin. But if you have a baby boy, keep a cloth handy to toss on the likely spurting fountain.*

◆ *Close nappy pins as soon as you take them off, for safety if baby grabs one.*

◆ *When pinning a nappy slide your fingers between the pin and your baby, to avoid accidentally pricking him.*

◆ *Clean any cream from your fingers before fastening the tapes on a disposable, or it won't stick.*

◆ *Don't leave your baby up on a changing surface even for a second. She may not give you any warning before she suddenly learns to turn over.*

◆ *If the nappy is absorbent enough not to leak and leave your baby wet and cold, and he doesn't have a rash, you needn't change him at night if he is just wet.*

Washing nappies

If you use washable nappies, good hygiene will help protect your baby from nappy rash. If soiled, hold the nappy in the toilet as you flush to rinse it through. Then drop it to soak, together with wet nappies, in a bucket containing a germicidal solution which you prepare every day. Keep a lid on the bucket until you are ready for the daily nappy wash. Wash nappies separately from other clothes on a regular wash programme, preferably with a non-biological detergent since biological solutions may irritate your baby's skin. Dry and air nappies thoroughly before use.

Changing time

You need a flat, firm surface for changing your baby. A padded changing mat which sponges off easily makes the job portable, but you could use a folded towel on the floor or the top of a chest of drawers. Have to hand everything you will need, so that you won't have to leave your baby for an instant once you've started. You might like to have one permanent changing station, and another basket or bag with everything in it for easy changing in other rooms.

Depending on what type of nappy you use, you will need a clean nappy, liner, waterproof and so on. You also need cotton wool, a bowl of warm water, baby lotion or vegetable oil and possibly a barrier cream. If there has been any leakage, you will need a change of clothes. For an older baby, you will appreciate a toy or interesting object to distract your baby from trying to escape the whole process.

Lay your baby on her back, and unfasten lower clothing. If wearing socks or bootees, it's a good idea to remove them because she may well kick into the dirty nappy. Using one hand hold her ankles with one finger between to stop them rubbing together, lift her legs and slide clothing under her back well up out of the way.

Unfasten the dirty nappy and if it is soiled use the unsoiled front part of the nappy to wipe away as much of the faeces as you can. Then fold the nappy over and lay it aside.

If your baby is just wet, plain water is all you need for wiping the nappy area. For a young baby cotton wool balls are softest on delicate skin, but after several weeks you could use ordinary toilet roll. If soiled, water may be enough but you might find it easier cleaning the faeces off with a little baby lotion or a natural vegetable oil such as almond oil.

To clean a baby girl, always wipe from front to back to prevent bacteria getting into the vagina. Never open the inner lips of the vulva to clean inside, as the vagina is self-cleaning, but just clean the exposed genitals. You may need to gently spread the vulva to wipe clean.

For a baby boy, wipe clean around the penis and then clean the genitals. Again, clean only the exposed areas and don't pull the foreskin back. It will probably be at least three or four years before the foreskin is loose enough to pull back for cleaning underneath and trying to do it too soon may cause small tears which result in adhesions. Circumcision, the surgical removal of the foreskin, is sometimes performed on baby boys as a religious practice but is very rarely necessary on medical or hygiene grounds, and never necessary on babies.

Chloe had a terrible case of thrush and the only way to clear it was to use terries for a week for the air to circulate. When the week was up I thought "Thank God". Disposables are so much easier, though I think they're hideously expensive – it's more than the child allowance just for nappies. We'd like to live an eco-friendly life, but we excuse ourselves by saying "Oh, well, we'll plant a couple of trees". RACHEL

When the genital area is clean, lift your baby's legs and clean the bottom. Then pat the whole area dry, paying special attention to the leg creases which could become sore if left damp. A barrier cream is not generally necessary, but if your baby has very sensitive skin or has nappy rash you could apply a soothing and protective nappy cream. Don't use baby powder, which is breathed into your baby's lungs and tends to cake in the creases leading to soreness.

Now you can put on a clean nappy and dress your baby again. Deal with the used nappy and then carefully wash your hands.

A fun time?

How your baby reacts to being changed will vary as she grows. Ideally, as with all the jobs of caring for a baby, it provides a chance for you to spend time together, chatting and being sociable. But many new babies hate being uncovered, understandably since they are used to the close all-over contact of the womb. Talk to your baby as you change her and reassure her. But if she is fretful and obviously unhappy at the process, just work as gently and efficiently as you can, to complete the job quickly and get her happily dressed and held again.

Later on she may enjoy a chat with you as you change her, and like the feeling of freedom in being without her nappy. If she is happy being undressed, leave her for a while to kick in the air – it's good exercise for her and good for the nappy area to be exposed to air.

Once your baby has learned to roll over and especially once she has become a mobile crawler or scooter, you have another job to do in keeping her still long enough to be changed. You could hang a colourful mobile above your changing area. Talking to her to keep her attention helps, especially if you produce an interesting toy at the right moment. By nine or ten months she might even like to 'help', holding a lotion bottle until you ask her for it.

Nappy rash

However careful you are, there is no foolproof prevention for nappy rash (see page 74). Some babies have much more sensitive skin than others, but there

73

TYPES OF NAPPY RASH

Ammonia dermatitis: *A red rash in the nappy area, starting around the genitals. You may notice the strong smell of ammonia on the nappy.*
Caused by: *Ammonia formed from bacteria acting on urine.*
What to do: *More frequent changes; bathe the area well; expose to air; do not use soap which can dry the skin; use one-way liners or disposables; use a soothing barrier cream.*

Thrush: *A painful red rash which starts around the anus and spreads on the buttocks, tending to be worse in creases. Thrush can also appear in the mouth as white spots and causes pain and difficulty in feeding.*
Caused by: Candida albicans *fungal infection.*
What to do: *See your doctor, who will probably prescribe an anti-fungal cream and perhaps medicine to take by mouth; dry carefully and expose the skin to air.*

Sore in creases: *Red or broken skin in leg creases.*
Caused by: *Damp in creases after changing or bath.*
What to do: *Pat dry carefully – don't rub delicate skin; expose to air; don't use powder, but soothing cream may help.*

Persistent rash: *Rash which doesn't clear with usual measures.*
Caused by: *Possibly lanolin or other substance in soaps, lotions or baby wipes, either through reaction of sensitive skin or disturbance of the natural oil balance of the skin.*
What to do: *Avoid use of all products except water and a natural vegetable oil.*

---

may be times when any baby develops a rash. To avoid a rash or limit its severity, the principles of frequent changes, exposure to fresh air and avoiding plastic as far as possible will make it more difficult for the culprit bacteria to work on the urine to form the stinging ammonia. If you use cloth nappies, using one-way liners or a temporary change to disposables might help clear up a rash. Or you could try rinsing nappies in a mild vinegar solution (1 cup to 4.5 litres/1 gallon of water), since the slight acidity slows down bacteria and neutralizes ammonia.

WASHING AND BATHING

You may feel that for you yourself sometimes nothing else can be as refreshing and soothing as slipping into a bath, and that getting clean becomes hardly more than a useful by-product of the pleasant time you have. Bathing your baby, too, can be a pleasure for you both – relaxing and, once splashing and pouring are discovered, great fun.

For your young baby

A new baby doesn't get very dirty, except for the face and neck from dribbled milk and the nappy area. So a daily full bath is not really necessary. 'Topping and tailing' – cleaning face and bottom – once or twice a day, and a more full wash every couple of days is sufficient. Some babies take to being surrounded by water right from the start, while others may be unhappy and not enjoy a bath for several weeks. If your baby cries and seems frightened in the bath, there is no need to use a bath at all but instead give a sponge bath on your lap. Or your baby may feel more secure if she has a bath with you, so she is held and supported throughout.

For your older baby

As your baby grows, a daily bath becomes more necessary. Once on solids, bits of food from hair to feet is not unusual and when she is mobile she will get grubby from active life at ground level. Arrange bathtime to suit yourself, but many parents like to bathe their baby in the evening, before the last feed. It can be a pleasant time for the father to spend with the baby and gives the mother a break if she has been providing care all day. A routine evening bath also helps relax your baby and signals bedtime.

Before she is able to sit up, your baby may discover that by arching her back and kicking she is able to

Supporting your baby's head with your forearm while your hand keeps a firm grip on his shoulder and arm leaves your other hand free for washing your baby while he enjoys lying, kicking or splashing in the warm water.

make huge splashes and bathtime fun takes on a whole new dimension. Once sitting in the bath, she will enjoy not only splashing but also playing with a variety of bath toys and familiar objects which behave differently in water. Floating, sinking, bottles that you can fill with water and squirt for her, and things which pour all become sources of exploration.

Water, however shallow, is always a source of danger so never leave your baby unattended. She could easily slip under or try to stand and fall. You should also keep a hand on her constantly until she is thoroughly reliable at sitting, because if she topples and goes under it can give her a bad fright and put her off water. It is a good idea to provide a bath mat to reduce the risk of your baby slipping.

Top and tail

For a quick cleaning of face, hands and bottom, you need warm water (previously boiled for a newborn), cotton wool, a towel and nappy changing things. Using a separate piece of moistened cotton wool for each eye, wipe from the middle outwards. Wipe around each ear and the outside ear, but do not clean inside the ears or put anything in them. Wipe the rest of the face, including creases under the chin, to remove any milk which will irritate the skin. Dry carefully by patting gently. Wipe the hands, dry and then remove your baby's nappy and clean as in any nappy change.

Sponge bath

For a sponge bath, you can wash your baby on a changing mat, or held on a towel on your lap. You will need a basin of water, cotton wool, face cloth, soap, shampoo, a towel and nappy changing things. Clean your baby's face as

The bath becomes an exciting playground once your baby can sit up. Getting clean isn't nearly as interesting as watching the bubbles, trying to catch the floating toy, making huge splashes, and pouring water from an assortment of cups and bottles.

BATHING TIPS

♦ *Make sure you have everything you will need within easy reach before you begin.*

♦ *Use a non-slip mat or a flannel or small towel in the bottom of the bath to keep your baby from sliding.*

♦ *Have a jug of hot water ready to top up the baby bath if it has cooled off too much before you are ready for it.*

♦ *Keep dry nappies, towel and a change of clothes handy but beyond splashing distance.*

♦ *If your baby doesn't like the feeling of water being poured over her head, rinse instead with a wet flannel, or scoop water onto her head with your hand.*

♦ *In the bathtub don't pull the plug until after your baby is out of the bath, as the noise and water leaving might frighten her.*

above, then remove clothes from the top of her body while the bottom stays dressed. Gently soap the front of her body, then rinse with the facecloth and carefully pat dry. Sitting her up and leaning her on your arm, repeat on her back. If you want to shampoo her hair, wet it with the cloth, lather and rinse well with the wet cloth. Then put on your baby's vest, remove the lower clothing and clean the nappy area. Finally wash legs and feet and dress her.

Giving a bath

To give your baby a bath, first gather everything you will need since you won't be able to leave her once you have begun. You can use a plastic baby bath, which can be carried into any room – but be careful of your back, bending your knees and not your back as you lift it and put it down. Or you can use a bathroom or kitchen sink, which may have convenient counter space. Move taps out of the way or wrap with a flannel. You will need the same items as for a sponge bath.

Fill the bath only a few inches deep. The water should be comfortably warm, probably not as warm as you would like a bath for yourself. Always check with your elbow that it is about your body temperature before putting your baby in the water.

First remove your baby's nappy and clean the nappy area. Then undress her, wrap her in a towel and clean her face. A young baby gets cold quite quickly in a bath, so to keep the time in the water short you can shampoo her hair before putting her in. Hold her with her legs under your arm, as your forearm supports her back and your hand holds her head. With her head over the bath, wet, shampoo and rinse her hair (see overleaf). With an older baby you can shampoo her while in the bath.

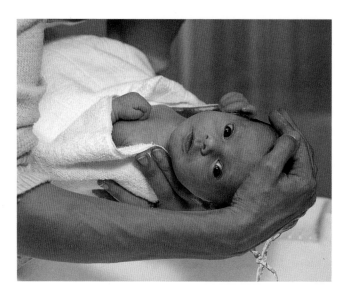

To keep your baby warm while you wash his hair, keep him wrapped snugly while you hold him with his head over the baby bath or basin to shampoo and rinse his hair. Then pat his head dry before continuing with the full bath.

To lower your baby into the bath, reach under her shoulders with your left hand (if you are right-handed), so your forearm supports her while your hand firmly grasps her shoulder and arm on the far side. With the other hand, lift her bottom as you firmly hold one thigh, and then lower her slowly into the bath. Talk to her to reassure her as she feels the water. Your left hand maintains a grip at all times, while the right hand will be free to wash your baby (see page 75). When she is clean and rinsed, lift her out on to a large dry towel, and wrap her quickly. Pat dry, being especially careful in the creases.

Sharing a bath

Even with a very young baby you might like to wash her in the bathtub with you. You may both enjoy the skin-to-skin contact, and she may feel more relaxed resting on your lap in the bath. It is easier if your partner hands your baby to you once you are already in the water, and takes her from you and wraps her in a towel when you are finished. It is possible to manage on your own, though. Clean your baby's face and nappy area, wrap her in a towel and lie her on the floor beside the bath while you get into the bath. Kneeling in the bath, pick her up and settle into the bath together. When you are ready to get out, kneel up and lower her on to the waiting towel, wrapping her before you step out.

Care of:

Hair: However little hair your baby has, it's a good idea to brush daily with a very soft brush to stimulate circulation in the scalp. Washing the hair needn't be done at every bath, but done once or twice a week using a gentle non-sting shampoo will keep it clean and may help avoid cradle cap. Don't be afraid of washing over the soft spots, which are covered with a tough membrane.

Nails: A young baby can easily scratch herself with long fingernails, so they need to be kept trimmed. You could use nail clippers, but special blunt-ended nail scissors are best. Cut finger nails in a slightly rounded shape; toe nails should be cut straight across. After a bath the nails are soft and easy to cut, or you might prefer to cut them while your baby is asleep so she won't jerk.

Ears and nose: Both the ears and nose are self-cleaning, so there is no need to try to clean inside them and you could do damage by poking anything into them. Just wipe away anything which appears on the outside.

DRESSING YOUR BABY

As with most aspects of baby care, dressing your baby has, along with its practical side, the opportunity for fun. Enjoy choosing clothes to make your baby look just so, handling your baby and getting to know him.

Temperature

The main purpose of clothing is to keep us warm, and keeping a baby comfortably dressed for the surrounding temperature is especially important. Your baby is able to keep his body temperature warm enough, so resist the tendency to overdress him, which is as harmful as underdressing. What babies can't do very effectively is alter body temperatures quickly to compensate for rapid temperature changes around them. So your baby might need layers adding or removing as you go from room to room or as temperatures change.

In general, your baby will be warm enough in the same number of layers

---

DRESSING

◆ *Buy three-months size clothes rather than newborn, so they won't be outgrown as quickly.*

◆ *Don't buy too much. You may receive baby clothes as gifts, and you can always add things later.*

◆ *Babies like strong bright colours so don't choose all soft pastels.*

◆ *All-in-one vests with poppers between the legs keep vests from riding up and exposing your baby's midriff.*

◆ *A shawl is useful for wrapping or covering your baby, but avoid lacy patterns with holes which can catch tiny fingers.*

◆ *Take a complete change of clothes for your baby when you go out.*

◆ *Both parents can dress their baby. To build confidence, let your partner get on with it in his own way, even if you're not keen on his combination of clothes. Your baby doesn't mind how he looks, but loves having both parents involved.*

'Felicity went round in blue for the first year because I'd inherited baby clothes from my sister, and everyone said "What's his name?" But I didn't want to dress her up, because she was a sicky baby and in the end I just gave up. And dresses aren't very practical anyway. ' ANNE

that you are wearing. To check that he is warm but not too hot, you can feel the back of his neck or on his body. He should feel a bit warm, but not sweaty. Don't go by hands and feet, which might feel a bit cooler even when he is warm enough.

First clothes

New babies usually don't like being dressed much, so choose clothes which make dressing him easy, as well as being comfortable and simple to care for.

Your baby will be more comfortable in clothes made of natural fibres which 'breathe', with cotton next to the skin. A small percentage of synthetic fibre with cotton may make the clothes easy-care, drying well with no need to iron.

Look for clothes which open at the front for ease of changing, and with poppers or Velcro for easy fastening. Stretchy clothes are also easier to use and probably more comfortable for your baby. Anything which must go over the head should have a wide neck opening, either with an envelope neck or poppers which open along the shoulder.

For a young baby, stretchsuits are an excellent wardrobe basic because they are comfortable to wear, easy to launder and use, and can be used with other thin layers such as vests and cardigans. They can be worn day and night, although you may prefer nightgowns which make night changes easier. Avoid open-weave knitwear as young babies tend to trap their fingers in the holes, and garments with fringes or ribbons which your baby may suck. Keep an eye on buttons to make sure they are firmly sewn on – loose buttons present a potential choking hazard.

A young baby grows quickly, so don't buy much in the first size. Your baby won't mind being dressed in slightly over-large clothes for the short time until he grows into them. Do keep an eye on fit. Pressure on tiny feet from stretchsuits which are too short or too-small socks can damage the soft bones of the feet, so make sure there is plenty of room. To lengthen the life of a stretchsuit, you can cut off the feet and use socks with it instead.

Active clothes

Once your baby has begun to crawl, tougher clothes which offer protection to knees, and withstand the beating they will take, are needed. Beware of dresses for a girl, which will frustrate her as they catch under her knees and stop her crawling. Dungarees and tracksuits are a better bet and can be bright and decorative as well as functional.

For a baby beginning to walk clothes still need to be sturdy, as well as loose enough to allow comfortable free movement. Layers which can be added or taken off remain a good idea, as your baby will warm up when he is active.

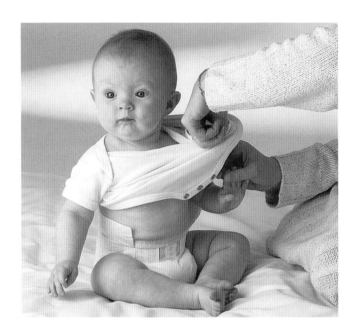

You soon become adept at dressing your baby, learning tricks like gathering up a shirt and stretching the neck wide to slip it over your baby's head, and reaching into the sleeve to draw her hand through. Before long, she'll be helping you, too.

Sun protection

In warm weather it is lovely for a baby to enjoy being outdoors, but guard carefully against sun exposure. Your baby's skin does not have much pigment to protect it against the sun's radiation and will burn and be damaged very quickly. Babies under six months should never be exposed to direct sunlight for any length of time, and in the sun must be well-covered by clothes and a hat with a brim. Older babies should wear a hat, UV protective clothing or a T-shirt and a high-factor sunscreen.

Dressing your young baby

You can dress your baby as he lies on his back, or sitting up on your lap. Because he probably doesn't like to be completely exposed, wrap him in a towel if he's just had a bath; otherwise keep him partly dressed while you work on one thing at a time.

He won't like clothes being pulled over his head and drawn over his face, so be careful as you take vests or tops over his head. To remove a vest, pull the body of the vest up and stretch the armholes open as you bend his elbows to guide his arms out first. Gather up the vest, stretching the neck hole open wide. Reassure him as you slip it over the front, being careful not to touch his face. Then slide it out from under his neck. When you put a vest on, concertina it up and stretch the neck hole open. Put it on over the back of your baby's head, then stretch it wide to clear his face as you pull it forward.

To put sleeves on, reach into the sleeve from the wrong end, grasp your baby's hand and slip the sleeve on. With a stretchsuit or cardigan, you can

concertina the sleeve, guide your baby's hand through, and straighten the sleeve along his arm.

To put on a stretchsuit, open it up fully and lie your baby on it. Put on the arms first then fasten the poppers for the front and legs.

Protection from the sun's harmful rays is important with your baby's delicate skin. Use cool clothing and sun-barrier cream.

Dressing your older baby

By the time your baby is a few months old you may be surprised to find him suddenly helping you with dressing. Instead of being passively moved, he will stretch his arm to push it through a sleeve. Participation like this is the first step in eventually being able to dress himself, so do encourage him to take part. Talk to him about what you are doing, step by step: 'Let's have your hand. Push...good. Now the other one.' It takes longer to involve him, especially if he becomes distracted by wanting to play with other things or get away, but you will both enjoy it and you will be teaching him self-reliance if you do it together rather than you just forcing it on him without his involvement or even against his will.

He will probably prefer you to dress him as he sits or stands. Hold him on your lap or between your knees as you kneel, and he can stand up as you pull up pants or trousers. By 18 months, he may be able to pull off some of his clothes by himself and may push his feet into shoes. You can sit him on a step and arrange his shoes in front of him for him to put his feet into.

QUESTIONS AND ANSWERS

Q: My baby has cradle cap, even though I keep his hair clean. How can I clear it up, and prevent it coming back?

A: Cradle cap is a common skin condition where dry scaly crusts form on the scalp, caused by overproduction from immature oil glands in the scalp. It is harmless, but unsightly, so you will probably want to remove any crusts which form. Ordinary shampoo has little effect. Never try to pick the crusts off, as you could tear the skin beneath and could cause infection. The crusts can be softened by rubbing a little baby oil or olive oil into the scalp and leaving it for several hours or overnight. Then with a fine-toothed comb you can gently remove the crusts, and follow with a thorough shampoo. Washing now and then with a medicated shampoo may help prevent cradle cap, but it does tend to come back so just use the same procedure again.

Q: When I put a soft wool cardigan on my baby her skin went red. Does this mean she is allergic to wool?

A: Some young babies are sensitive to wool and may become irritated, but this is not an allergy. You could probably use wool if it is not in direct contact with your baby's skin and if she wears cotton beneath. Alternatively, you could choose a cardigan made from synthetic yarn instead.

Q: Should I buy shoes for my baby now that she is beginning to pull herself up to stand?

A: Feet grow most healthily when they are not restrained in shoes and even slight distortions in the soft bones early in life can cause problems later on. Socks or bootees with plenty of room are all your baby needs until she begins to walk. Even then, it is advisable to wait until your baby has been walking for several weeks before buying her first pair of shoes. For indoors, soft fabric boots with grip on the sole are a good choice.

When buying shoes be sure your baby is carefully fitted by a trained fitter who checks both length and width, that the foot does not slip in the shoe and is not restricted. Choose shoes with non-slip soles which are flexible, not rigid. There are many attractive, fashionable baby shoe styles available, but do put foot health first.

Q: When will my baby be ready to start potty training?

A: He will hardly be a baby at all by the time he is ready to start, but more into the toddler stage. It is possible for you to learn when your baby is likely to fill his nappy, and put him on the potty at those times, but he won't be ready to learn for himself for some time. He has to mature enough to notice what is happening, then to be aware in advance and to signal to you that he needs the potty in time to get there. Most children are between 18 months and two-and-a-half years before all these things come together.

6

Sleep

' People sometimes ask me, "Is she a good baby?" I know that what they really mean is does she sleep a lot? Well, of course she's good – it goes without saying that all babies are good. But no, she doesn't sleep nearly as much as I wish she would, and I'm absolutely exhausted. '

PARENTS' EXPECTATIONS

Few aspects of life with a baby have as much impact as the question of sleep – when your baby sleeps, how much she sleeps and what happens when she doesn't. Her sleep pattern becomes the centre which you and the rest of your family range yourselves around, adjusting your own sleep and activity to fit.

How difficult that adjustment is for you is partly determined by what you expect. Some parents expect a baby to wake at intervals through the night for a feed, continuing once or twice a night for several months. Though adjusting sleep patterns is never easy and they probably have times of feeling very tired themselves, they will still take it in their stride and adapt around that pattern. It will be harder for parents who expect that after the first few weeks their baby will allow them peaceful evenings together, followed by an uninterrupted night's sleep. Instead of putting their attention on how to make things as easy for themselves as possible in the circumstances, they will be constantly frustrated at being in those circumstances at all.

There *are* some ways parents can influence a baby's sleep: in how you settle her to bed and encourage the idea that night-time is for sleep. But your influence does not extend to the overall amount your child sleeps. So the key is in accepting the basic outline of your baby's sleep and then trying to fit in as restfully for yourself as possible.

HOW MUCH SLEEP DOES A BABY NEED?

The short answer is your baby needs just the amount of sleep she is getting. She will sleep neither less nor more than she actually needs. If you are lucky, your baby will sleep enough for you, too, to get enough rest, but you might have the bad luck to find that your baby needs very little sleep at all. As a newborn your baby may sleep as little as eight hours a day or as much as 16 or 20. As she grows her need for sleep will change, both in total amount and in when she sleeps. She may well sleep less as she goes through the first 12 months or so, but the range of normal variation is so wide that there is no point talking about what to expect 'on average'. Your baby is not an average, but an individual.

WHERE SHOULD A BABY SLEEP?

A young baby is adaptable, and needn't have one particular place to sleep. The room should be comfortably warm, without draughts. A cradle, basket or pram is easily portable and a good size for a young baby. If you prefer to use a cot, you should lie your baby in the 'feet to foot' position – that is on her back, tucked in with her feet to the foot of the cot. This way there is no danger of her slipping under the covers and becoming too hot. Babies under a year should not have cot bumpers or pillows.

While you may want to bring your baby into bed with you while you feed him, especially if you are breastfeeding, it is probably best not to bring a small baby into bed to sleep with you. Apart from the fact that you will probably disturb each other's sleep, there is also a very slight danger that you or your partner could roll over on your baby. A better alternative is to let your baby sleep in a crib or cot pushed up close to your bed. Then you can deal with her easily in the night.

' Her sleep is perfect. She has her last feed around seven at night, and she'll sleep through to the next morning around seven. Often I come in around half past seven and she's awake, just lying there contented thinking I'm coming, with a big smile on her face. '
HELEN

Many parents like to move their babies into a separate room after several weeks, when the sleeping spells at night have grown longer. But for some, a separate room right from the beginning is a good choice. If you are a light sleeper and find yourself waking at every little murmur, or not able to get back to sleep after a feed as you listen to your baby's rustles and breathing, it might be a better idea to put your baby in a nearby room for the night.

All children differ in how much sleep they require. Although you cannot change your baby's individual need for sleep, there are nevertheless ways in which you can influence his sleep pattern to fit in more with your routine.

In the daytime in warm weather your baby can sleep outside. Make sure her pram is well-shaded and not in direct sun and has good air circulation; use a cat net over the pram or basket.

CHANGING SLEEP PATTERNS

Babies differ in their need for sleep so don't blame yourself if your baby doesn't seem to sleep much. You're not doing anything wrong – it's just her individual temperament.

Birth to six months

In the first few days of life your baby may sleep for long periods or irregular short spells. After feeding is established she will fall into something of a rhythm of sleeping and feeding. She may tend to sleep until she wakes up hungry, around every two to four hours. But babies who require less sleep may wake before they are hungry, or stay awake after feeds rather than dropping off when their bellies are full.

A young baby usually sleeps through background noise and it is a good idea to carry on with normal household noise rather than get your baby used to complete silence for sleeping. She may be wakened, though, by sudden noises such as a shout or a door banging.

At first she will have no sense of day and night and will be as wakeful at night as during the day. Gradually, as you keep the room darkened at night, stay quiet and settle her back as quickly as possible into bed, she will recognize the contrast with the sociability and activity of daytime and begin to have more of her wakeful hours in the day and sleep at night.

This doesn't mean sleeping through the night, though. At three months the majority of babies are still awake for some time during the night, and this is likely to continue for several more months.

Six to 12 months

Your baby is now more active and involved in everything around her, and she doesn't want to be separated from you – so she may begin to protest at going to bed even when she is tired. If you settle her calmly with a regular routine, she will probably cry for only a couple of minutes when you put her to bed. Don't leave her to cry if she is really upset. You will soon learn the difference between a real cry and a grizzly protest which will fade away. Once she can sit up or pull herself up to stand, she may need settling again once she is ready to go to sleep. If you go in, don't pick her up right away, but lie her down, pat her soothingly and gently but firmly let her know it is time to sleep.

Periods of deep sleep are shorter now and she may surface at intervals, making small noises and squirming before she settles again. A baby alarm which transmits to you every little mutter can do you a disservice now. If you go to her when she is at this stage rather than waiting until she is fully awake, you are training her to continue waking and wanting attention at frequent intervals. Instead, wait and see if she settles by herself again.

You can leave some toys and board books at the foot of your baby's cot, and when she wakes she may play and babble for some time.

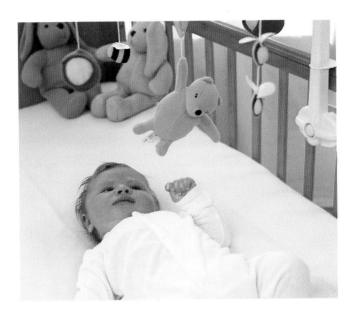

Between the ages of three to six months your baby is likely to be spending more time awake, not just waking to be fed. While he is awake he is learning about the world around him, and he is able to amuse himself for short periods by looking at things around him, reaching and touching. If he has a crib mobile or toys dangling over his cot, he may be interested and entertained and not cry for you as soon as he wakes.

Twelve to 18 months

By now your baby is likely to be sleeping less during the day, perhaps having settled on one long midday nap. An established settling routine will come into its own now, as the familiar cuddle, lullaby and tucking in is a clear signal that it's time to go to sleep. About one baby in five is still waking regularly during the night, but many will normally sleep through and wake only at times of unusual stress such as illness or teething. On waking she may not cry at all, but may call you and then wait patiently for you to appear.

A ROUTINE LIFE?

Having a routine to your days with your baby can be useful, because you will be organizing a lot of your life around when your baby needs to sleep. But rather than try to impose a routine, take your cue from your baby. She will establish patterns in her waking and sleeping and if you keep track for a few days you may find it is more regular than you realized. You can plan shopping, visits to friends, or household jobs around or during sleep times.

For a young baby surroundings and routine aren't very important and she will readily sleep somewhere else if you go out for the evening. As she gets older, though, she becomes more fixed on her own routine and may find it harder to settle and sleep away from her familiar patterns and environment. Arranging your activities so that she is at home to sleep encourages regularity and a peaceful life, and may be the most realistic approach to this time.

There are two problems with living by a baby's routine. One is that it doesn't stay the same – no sooner have you got used to it than it shifts. If you

'*Everything was fine until Andrew got a viral infection at seven months, and for weeks he was feverish in the night and woke frequently or sometimes we had to wake him to give him plenty of fluids. That set a pattern, and when he was over the infection he kept waking a lot. It really stopped only when we moved him out of his cot into a bed with the side up, and that seemed to break the pattern.* ' PETER

remain flexible and are prepared to rearrange your schedule it will avoid some frustrations.

The other problem with a routine is that it can become too confining. You have other interests and responsibilities which may not fit in. You may need to go out and your baby isn't awake yet. Or perhaps her long afternoon nap means she is wide awake in the evening, and you would rather she went to bed earlier to leave you some free time in the evening. You needn't be a slave to your baby's routine, but can expect her to be a bit flexible, too.

There is no harm in waking your baby a bit early from her sleep, especially if you think she is near to waking in any case. She may be irritable and need some time to come round, so wake her in good time to rouse her gently. If you want to change the time of a nap, sometimes rearranging other parts of her day will do the trick. You could give her lunch earlier, to move the afternoon nap forward. Being outside often keeps a baby awake and stimulated and ready for sleep on coming back inside, so you could try taking her out as a way of altering her nap pattern.

SETTLING YOUR BABY TO SLEEP

As soon as you notice your baby is tired, it's time to settle him to sleep. If you wait longer, he may become overtired and distressed and it will be harder for him to fall asleep. First be sure that all his physical needs are met – that he's not hungry or thirsty, he is comfortable with a clean nappy and not too hot or cold. Then a calm, fairly quiet atmosphere will help him wind down to sleep.

Young babies often fall asleep during a feed, and then you can just lie him down. But it's probably best not to let him become dependent on falling asleep at the breast or bottle, because it can cause trouble later. If he will go to sleep only during a feed, when he surfaces from sleep – as we all do at intervals during the night – he will wonder where he is and cry for the breast or bottle again, rather than just drifting off to sleep again. So it's best to let him become drowsy and ready for sleep, but be still awake when he's put to bed.

Soothing to sleep

There are several time-honoured techniques for soothing your baby. One is to use rhythmic movement. Rocking your baby in a rocking chair, rolling him back and forth in his pram, going for a walk with him in a sling, walking about with him as you gently bounce up and down, holding him as you stand and sway or taking him for a car ride are all types of rhythmic movement.

He may also settle more easily with rhythmic sound. Sing him a song – it can be anything, not just the traditional lullabies and he won't mind at all if you haven't got a great singing voice! You can combine the singing with rocking and let both gradually slow and quieten, until they nearly fade away and then finally stop. You can also buy soothing tapes of womb sounds, which combine the heartbeat and whooshing sounds of life before birth. These seem to work best if they are started within the first weeks of life, before he forgets. Other shapeless sounds work, too, such as a radio tuned so it is not on a station or the motor noise of a vacuum cleaner.

Comforters

Your baby may like to have a comforter, a familiar object to which he becomes attached, to help him to sleep. He may fasten his affection on to a particular blanket or a cuddly toy and the attachment can last for years so that he is unable to sleep without it. Even taking it away for washing causes problems, because when it reappears it looks and smells different. If your child has a special comforter don't take it away but wait until he outgrows wanting it, however tattered it has become. Be sure to take it when you are away from home, and to tell babysitters about its importance so it isn't left out of the cot.

Some babies become attached to a dummy and will only sleep if they have it in their mouths. There are problems here, such as maintaining a supply of clean dummies, getting up in the night to replace a dummy which has fallen out of a baby's mouth and eventually dropping the habit. Some babies, though, have a great desire to suck and are only satisfied and sleepy with something in their mouths, so you will have to weigh up the pros and cons for your baby.

Other babies learn early on – possibly even in the womb – to suck their thumbs or fingers, which as a soothing habit has the advantage that they

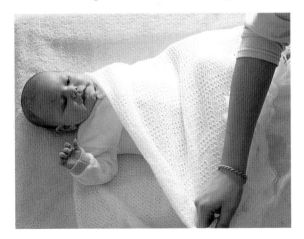

Many young babies like to be swaddled before being laid down to sleep, as it seems to help them feel more held and secure. Use a soft cloth or shawl to enclose legs and body, but leave arms free. After a few weeks your baby will want her legs free to move during sleep, but in the beginning it can ease falling asleep.

Some babies fall asleep and rest more peacefully while cuddling a special security object. You can't predict whether your baby will develop such an attachment, or what object she may choose – but whether it's a lovely soft toy or a tatty piece of blanket, it's just as important to her.

control it themselves. However, this can also be a difficult habit to break, but that may be something you will have to face when the time comes.

Positions for sleeping

A young baby should be placed on his back when laid down to sleep. Don't worry that he may be sick and choke if he is on his back. There is no evidence that this happens and he will turn his head to one side in any case.

Evidence about cot death shows that it is more common among babies who sleep on their stomachs, perhaps because of an increase in body temperature. So for a young baby it is best not to put him down on his stomach. By the time he is old enough to turn over by himself, it is safe to let him sleep in whatever position he prefers.

NIGHT-TIME

Once your baby is old enough and his feeds have settled into a pattern, to encourage peaceful nights an evening routine that marks the difference from daytime sleeps can be helpful. You may decide on a routine that involves a bath, then withdrawing to a quiet room for a look at a book together, a last feed and a cuddle.

Wakeful baby

A young baby who is awake at night for more than a quick feed and then back to sleep will have tired parents. The baby himself will not be tired, but simply doesn't need more sleep and may want company and stimulation during the night. If you have a wakeful baby you could try bringing your baby into your bed. He may be calmed by your presence and you may get more sleep.

Since your baby is fine, the important thing to work on is how you can manage. Rest when you can in the day and have early nights. But daytime rest doesn't completely make up for broken nights, so share the load with your partner. Your partner may have to get up for work in the morning, but so do you. If you are breastfeeding, the father can still do the nappy changing and walking the floor with the baby while you get back to sleep, and let you have an occasional lie-in in the morning. If you are bottlefeeding, you can take turns with night feeds, or have alternate nights on duty. Losing sleep with a baby is never easy, but having enough support can make the difference between coping and sinking into constant fatigue or depression.

Waking for feeds

Some babies continue to wake regularly during the night, long after they are on solid meals and one baby in five still wakes regularly through the second year of life.

You could try leaving him for a few minutes when he wakes to see if he goes back to sleep. The next step in trying to change the waking habit is that when you go to him, don't give him milk or juice, but just plain water or preferably nothing at all. Keep touching and contact to the minimum and settle him firmly back to bed as soon as possible.

If you have been giving him a breastfeed or bottle, this will seem a big shift to him and he is likely to protest. It might help to forewarn him. Even at less than one year old, your baby will understand some of what you say to him, as well as your tone of voice. You can tell him firmly as you settle him for sleep, 'No crying in the night. No milk in the night. Night is for sleeping.' When he wakes in the night, you can repeat this as you calmly but firmly tuck him up.

TIPS FOR SLEEP

◆ *For safety always put your baby down to sleep on his back with his feet at the foot of his cot.*

◆ *Pre-warming the crib or cot with a hot water-bottle can encourage sleep – but take it out before you put your baby down.*

◆ *Don't let your baby fall asleep with a bottle, because saliva slows down in sleep so the milk isn't rinsed away and can cause new teeth to decay; sugary drinks are even worse.*

◆ *Overheating in sleep is dangerous. Use a few light cellular blankets that you can add or take away, rather than duvets or baby nests. Don't overdress your baby for sleep and the room should be no warmer than that which you find comfortable.*

◆ *If you are getting on with jobs while your baby sleeps, stop and have 15 minutes' relaxation before you think he is likely to wake up.*

◆ *Allow extra time for settling your baby to sleep when you are going out. He'll know if you are trying to rush things and won't settle.*

If one parent normally handles the night wakings and a feed, it may help for the other parent to go instead since then your baby has less expectation of milk and will know that something has changed. Often a couple of nights of this routine is enough to convince a baby that what's on offer isn't worth waking up for.

You must be consistent if you have decided to make this change, since if you give in and offer a feed and cuddle you will have undone the lesson. If your baby is distressed by the change and cries for you, it will be terribly stressful for you to listen to. You need the support of your partner, or ask a friend or relative to come spend a couple of nights to give you moral support.

A checking routine will reassure both you and your baby that nothing terrible is happening. Leave him for five minutes and then you or your partner can go in and repeat the message that it's time to go to sleep. Leave again, for a few minutes longer this time. Continue in this pattern until your baby realizes nothing is to be gained from crying and falls asleep. Usually a night or two of this is all that will be needed for you all to enjoy very welcome nights of unbroken sleep.

When your baby wakes in the night, handle all activity in subdued light and with the minimum of interaction, so there is no sociable reward for being awake at night. Eventually your baby will understand that night is for sleeping and you can both get back to sleep as quickly as possible.

QUESTIONS AND ANSWERS

Q: At three months my baby had been waking only once or twice a night for a feed, but suddenly she is waking every couple of hours. Does this mean breastmilk isn't enough and she needs to start on solids?

A: No, she doesn't need to start solids yet. Four months is the earliest age recommended and six months is preferable. Your baby is probably in one of a number of growing spurts, which often come at around six weeks, three months and four and a half months; and a breastfed baby will tend to need feeds more often at these times for a few days. The extra stimulation will soon build up the milk supply. So stick with it and your baby should soon go back to sleeping for longer periods.

Q: At six in the morning my baby is awake and ready for action, and I'd really like to sleep another hour. Any suggestions?

A: A mobile or toys tied on to an elastic over the cot might keep your baby occupied for a while, especially if you put him to sleep on his back so he can see them easily on waking. A dim light in the room would also help on dark mornings. When he fusses for a feed, bring him into your bed and you can then doze on afterwards. Once he is able to sit up, leaving board books and toys in the cot will help him to entertain himself for a while. Change the toys, mobiles or pictures every few days, because he will be much more interested in something which is slightly different from the day before. Wakeful babies are often bright and curious and can become quite good at occupying themselves.

Q: My baby sleeps in a crib next to my bed and sometimes in the night I hear his breathing stop for a few seconds. When he's been sleeping longer than I expect, I have to go and check that he's still breathing. Can I do anything to protect him from cot death?

A: Every parent knows the fear that their baby may simply stop breathing in the night and it's made worse by the fact that we don't understand the causes of cot death and so can't completely prevent it. It can occur at any age up to 18 months or so, but most often between birth and five months. Fortunately it is rare and there are simple steps you can take which current research shows can reduce the risk. Try not to think too much about it and become over-anxious. It is normal for a baby of up to three months to have a breathing pattern of light panting followed by a pause lasting several seconds. Do reassure yourself by placing a hand on your baby if you are worried.

Important steps you can take are to get your baby used to sleeping on his back, rather than on his stomach and to ensure he is not overheated in his sleep from too warm a room and too many clothes or coverings. A smoke-free environment also reduces the risk, so ask any smokers to step outside. If your baby has a cold or other infection, see your doctor for medical advice and be especially careful about overheating. Some worry is natural, but if you find yourself very anxious talk to your health visitor or doctor.

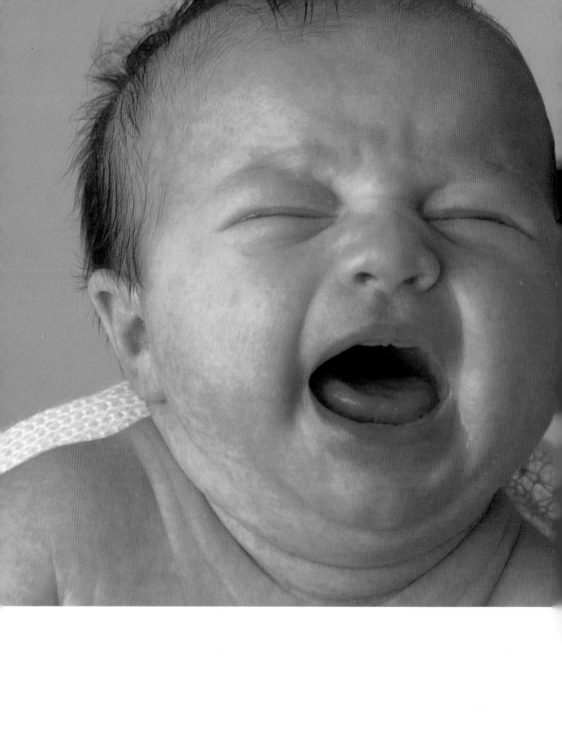

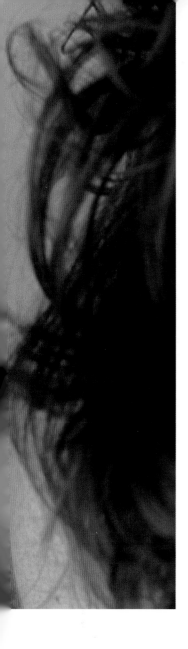

7

Crying

'*I've never been able to leave her to scream and resist the temptation of picking her up. When babies are tiny you feel you must be able to do something to comfort them. Even when nothing I did helped, I just kept thinking to myself this can only go on for so long.*'

CRYING TO COMMUNICATE

'How can there be a baby with no crying?' asks an old folk song, reflecting what we all know – babies and crying go together. But if a baby's cry is a natural and normal part of life, why does it have the power to drive parents to distraction like no other sound?

It's all part of nature's plan for human survival for you to have such a strong response to your baby's cry. If it didn't trigger you to action, trying everything you can think of to solve the problem and stop the crying, your baby might not have crucial needs met and his survival might be in question.

Crying is a new baby's only way of telling you that something is wrong. He doesn't know exactly what the problem is, but only that he is uncomfortable or in pain right now and so he expresses how he feels. It will be weeks and months before he learns the difference between feeling hungry, or cold, or frustrated and learns that you can and will help him. As he discovers other ways to communicate with you, his reliance on crying becomes less. How you respond to his cries from the beginning is part of the process of teaching him to trust that he will be all right, that you will respond to him, and that he needn't cry so much.

Follow your instinct

Within a couple of days of your baby's birth you will recognize his cry and your urge is to do something to get the crying to stop. This urge comes partly from tender concern for your baby's well-being and happiness, but the instinct to help him is more than that. A chemical reaction in your body also spurs you into action. Your baby's cry is a powerful stimulus which causes stress hormones to be automatically released into your bloodstream, with the effect of increasing your blood pressure, breathing rate and muscular tension. This feels uncomfortable and the more the crying goes on the more uncomfortable you feel. You *must* do something and if the crying doesn't stop you may end up feeling frantic and in tears yourself.

So your strong instinctive reaction is to try to find the cause of your baby's crying, put things right and have him calm and contented again. This is what makes you feel good and is exactly the reaction your baby needs. He wants you to help him when he cries, and needs to learn that the world is a good place to be and that he can trust in life and in you.

Spoiling the child?

If you do follow your instinct and pick up your baby when he cries, the comment may come that you are 'spoiling' him, or 'making a rod for your own back'. Leaving a baby to cry, however, doesn't discourage him from crying. If he is left, he becomes more unhappy and so cries more. He becomes unsettled and insecure because he expects no help arriving when he needs it, so as he grows older he is not contented and confident but continues to fuss and cry.

As her parents tune into her needs and her other signals – such as making sucking noises or rooting around with her mouth as a sign of hunger, or rubbing her eyes signalling tiredness – she may begin to cry less because her needs are met before she has to complain.

One study found that babies whose mothers respond quickly when they cry in the first three months of life cry less often, and for shorter periods, than those whose mothers delay or ignore crying. By four months, the promptly-seen-to babies are less likely to cry persistently, and at one year of age they are more independent and communicate in more ways other than crying.

From baby to toddler

A young baby cries to express his immediate needs, and those needs are frequent and to him feel strange and intense. He needs feeding, changing, he gets tired or overtense, he needs to be touched and held. Since he has so much to adjust to all at once in the sudden change from life in the womb, it's not surprising that he may cry quite often. He cries most when he is out of sight, sound and touch of his mother and the most effective way to settle him in the early weeks is to pick him up and feed him.

By about four months he is likely to cry less than before. Now he has other ways of communicating as he smiles and laughs with his parents, and a rhythm of care and understanding of each other's signals means he has less need to cry.

When he is eight months old, his crying spells are less frequent and usually clearly linked to what is

' When she was a few weeks old she had a pattern of crying for about a half hour every evening. I'd just let her cry, because it just seemed she needed a crying time, and it wasn't bad crying but stopping and starting. Now she can see more things in the window and on the wall and she's more contented. ' HEATHER

'*He went through a phase at 16 months of screaming at night, keeping us up all night and my sister said "You'll just have to leave him." So I lay on the floor of his room where he could see me and put cotton wool in my ears. He screamed for an hour and a quarter and then went to sleep. He cried less the next night and then it stopped. Being in his room but not doing anything, he knew where I was and I could see he wasn't biffing his head against the cot so it reassured me.* ' JANE

happening around him. He may be frustrated because he wants to do something he can't quite manage, he may be bored and cry because he wants your attention and company, or he may cry from fear when a stranger picks him up.

Between a year and 18 months, he has developed a much bigger range of ways to communicate with you, so he relies less on crying. He can use a few words and meaningful sounds, he points or uses other gestures and he shows his feelings through facial expressions. But he will still cry from frustration, either when he is not yet capable of something he wants to do or at being told 'no'. He will also cry at separation from you when you leave him.

WHY IS YOUR BABY CRYING?

Babies cry because something is wrong and they feel unhappy. By learning to interpret your baby's signals and respond promptly to her needs, you help her to become happy and confident about life.

Hunger

For a young baby hunger is a new and very unpleasant sensation and feels urgent. By the time she is a few months old, your baby can wait more patiently if she knows food is coming. An older baby or toddler has a less urgent appetite, but will still be fretful and demanding when hungry.

What to do: Feeding a young baby is the most successful way to settle her. If you are breastfeeding, you can offer the breast first whenever she cries. If she is not hungry she either won't be interested, or will be sucking more for the comfort than food. Don't worry about overfeeding – she may take just the less filling foremilk. If you are bottlefeeding you can still offer a feed, but you have to be more careful about overfeeding. If your baby has recently had a feed you could still offer a bit more milk to help her settle, but don't let her take a whole feed.

Don't delay in feeding your baby when she is hungry, or she will become more upset and be difficult to settle for feeding when you are ready. If she is frantic she may swallow too much air with her feed, causing her to bring the milk back or have a tummy pain. You could try to stop or at least reduce the crying before a feed – she may be temporarily placated if you rock her or bounce her gently up and down, pat her back and talk to her as you prepare her feed.

Need for contact

Your baby's need for the security of contact with a loving caretaker is of supreme importance. She may cry because she can't see or hear you, or she may need to be held and feel the reassurance of your presence. She is not trying to manipulate you, but is just expressing a real need.

What to do: Pick her up – being held may be all she needs, and you can get used to doing all sorts of household jobs with one arm. You can also use a baby sling, so she is in contact with you and you still have both arms free to get on with your work.

Overstimulation

A baby's senses can easily become overloaded by all the sights and sounds around them, even by being talked to and looked at, held and rocked. A young baby is not able to tune out the stimulation and so can become very tense and stressed. It's ironic that at times like this the more you do to try to settle your baby, the worse it can become. It often happens towards the end of the day – you may notice your baby's body stiffening, pushing out with arms and legs and possibly crying more when you pick her up.

What to do: Reduce the stimulation for your baby. Darken the room, don't make eye contact with her or speak. Use only monotonous low sounds, like a 'shhhh, shhhh' or a low hum. Lie her down, rather than holding or rocking and if you touch her at all just place your hand on her quietly to convey the idea of stillness. Swaddling (see page 91) may help by limiting movement and keeping her still, even if she fights it at first. She may need to cry for a few minutes to release tension, so leaving her for a few minutes to see if she winds down may be the best thing to do.

Your baby needs a lot of physical contact with you, but sometimes even being held is tiring and can leave a baby's nerves fraught. You need to decide whether contact like holding and rocking is helping or stillness is needed.

Discomfort

Clothes which pull, being too hot or cold, having wind, teething, needing a nappy change are all things which may make your baby uncomfortable. It's uncertain whether babies really mind being wet – one study found that babies who were picked up, changed and had the same wet nappy put back on settled just as happily as those who were given a dry nappy. Perhaps being handled was more important than being dry. A soiled nappy is more likely to cause irritation and may make your baby cry.

What to do: Try to discover the problem, and correct it. If it isn't apparent, it's a matter of trial and error and ruling out possible problems. For teething, a ring to chew on which has been chilled in the refrigerator is soothing.

Illness or pain

A cry of pain is usually abrupt, often a loud cry followed by a silence as the baby draws breath to let out a scream. A loud intense wail with knees drawn up may suggest that the baby has colic, an abdominal pain which may be caused by cramps in the bowel (see page 105). The cry of a baby who is ill is usually less intense and may be low and moaning.

What to do: If the cause of pain is apparent, deal with it and soothe your baby. If your baby's cry doesn't sound right and you think she may be becoming ill, contact your doctor.

Boredom

The need to learn and experience is very strong and your baby may cry if she is left without anything to interest her.

What to do: Don't expect your baby to lie happily just because she is fed and comfortable. Put her in an infant seat where she can see you, take her outside,

SOOTHING A CRYING BABY

- ◆ *First pick her up and try feeding her.*
- ◆ *Walk around with her up on your shoulder, with a rhythmic dip in your step just when she takes a big breath in for another cry.*
- ◆ *Keep your movements calm and regular, not bouncing or jiggling.*
- ◆ *Put her in a sling and go for a walk.*
- ◆ *Swaddle her so she feels snug and secure.*
- ◆ *Hum or sing continuously, or play her some music.*
- ◆ *Rock her in a rocking chair, with a shawl wrapped around you both.*
- ◆ *Lie her down and rub or pat her back.*
- ◆ *Take her for a ride in the car.*
- ◆ *Have a bath together, followed by a gentle massage.*
- ◆ *Try a dummy if she is calmed by sucking.*

Sucking often brings comfort even when it has nothing to do with a feed. Babies may suck their fingers or thumbs, or a dummy. A breastfed baby may be comforted by sucking at the breast, even soon after a feed when he is not hungry.

hang toys where she can see and reach them. With an older baby, let her play near you and include her in what you are doing. Her attention span with objects may be short, but if you periodically get involved too, they take on a whole new aspect for her.

Frustration

Babies have a huge drive to accomplish things and may become frustrated when they want to reach the next stage which is just beyond their abilities. Being told 'no' is also frustrating and can lead to tears.

What to do: Tactful help and support at the right time can ward off frustration. Hold in place the toy which keeps falling over or move something just that bit more into her reach. If she persists in crying because she is simply incapable of doing something, you might be able to distract her attention into something else new and interesting. Distraction is also a good approach instead of having to directly tell her 'no'. You can avoid confrontation if you child-proof your house so there are not too many forbidden things around.

Becoming unwilling to be left with someone else so she cries when you try to leave is actually a sign of your baby growing in understanding – she realizes how important and special you are to her. Patience in preparing her may help.

Separation

Before about four months your baby will not cry if you leave her with someone else, but as she learns the difference between trusted people and strangers she may cry if you go away from her. At certain stages, especially when she is learning new skills, she will become more clinging.

What to do: Try not to leave your baby with strangers, but let her get to know people while you are there before she is left with them. Don't force her to go to someone when she doesn't want to. When you leave her, let her know you are going and that you will be back – an older baby or toddler can understand the meaning of 'back' – rather than sneaking out which will only make her more nervous about separation. Being patient when she needs security will help her be more independent in the long run.

STILL CRYING?

You may have located what you think is the problem, dealt with it and your baby is still crying. Now what? Sometimes your baby can be so worked up that he is not able to stop his crying, as if being upset is in itself upsetting him beyond whatever the original problem was. Then it's time to try soothing techniques which may help him unwind. Don't give up when one technique doesn't work, but try another. You are likely to feel worked up yourself by the crying, so take some deep breaths and try to calm yourself. If you are tense and upset your baby will feel it and become even more stressed. Luckily a lot of the soothing techniques like rocking and singing will calm you, too.

If nothing seems to help, ask your partner or someone else to take over. Often someone who is less emotionally involved will be more calm and your baby may settle. It will also give you a break. If no one is available, put your baby down in a safe place, close the door and leave him. Walk around in the garden, make yourself a cup of tea, or just sit down and breathe deeply and regularly. Your baby will not come to any harm and he may wind down and settle in a few minutes; if not at least you will be calmer and more able to help him when you go back.

COLIC

There is no clear agreement about the causes of colic or how to prevent it. It usually begins at around three weeks and stops at around three months. In regular crying spells, which may last for hours and occur most often in the evenings, the baby seems to be in intense pain as he screams, draws up his knees and often passes wind. Although the crying spells are extreme, the baby in all other respects is thriving normally and is generally well.

One opinion is that colic is caused by the immature gut going into spasm, perhaps triggered by a food sensitivity. For breastfeeding mothers, it may be worth trying to eliminate from your diet foods which may be the culprit, including chocolate, cabbage, onions, green peppers or milk products. For bottlefed babies, consult your doctor about whether a change of formula might help although this is unlikely.

Another view is that the problem is unlikely to be caused by food, since the crying tends to come at one time of day and not regularly after all feeds. It may instead be the result of tension – a sort of overdrive of your baby's immature nervous system – which would explain why the evening when you and your baby are both most tired and tense is the most common time. You could try to avoid tension in the evening by giving your baby a calming bath or massage in the afternoon to release tension, or going out for a walk. Look after yourself by doing any evening meal preparations earlier in the day so there is no pressure later, having a proper lunch and afternoon snack to give you energy and a rest in the afternoon. Use any soothing techniques for your baby, being sure to keep all your movements relaxed and slow rather than bouncing.

' From six in the evening until midnight she'd cry, feed and feed, throw up, then feed again, always struggling at the breast. It was awful, just what you don't need at the end of the day. We tried every brand of gripe water, and I actually went out to look for one with alcohol in it. Nothing worked, but then she suddenly stopped. ' PATRICIA

A matter of weeks seems like an eternity when your baby is crying, but at least colic does usually stop abruptly and it is in fact a short period out of all the time and pleasure you will share with your baby.

CRYING... AND CRYING

There are some babies who, regardless of what you do and how they are handled, cry more than most. It may look like colic, but it may not come at a certain time of day and may last beyond the time when colic usually stops. Exhausted and desperate to find a solution, the parents may receive much advice and try different approaches one after another, all to no effect. They may feel inadequate as parents, angry at the baby and guilty for feeling angry.

There is no magic solution to the problem, but it helps to understand that it is not your fault – you are not doing anything wrong. It isn't your baby's fault, either. Some babies just have a harder time adjusting in the beginning than others. In the early weeks, the type of labour and drugs used can affect a baby's level of tension and ability to settle. There is also evidence that if the mother suffered unusual levels of stress during pregnancy the baby is more likely to cry. It may be that prolonged exposure to the mother's stress hormones leaves the baby keyed up and it takes time for the tension to be released. Whatever the reason, some babies are more touchy and easily startled than others and consequently cry more.

Use whatever strategies you find most helpful to get you through this time, but don't wear yourselves out trying one thing after another. Concentrate on finding support for yourself: by sharing with a partner, arranging help for an hour or so to get out and have a break and talking things over with someone sympathetic to relieve your frustration. Your health visitor may be a source of support, as may a self-help group for parents of crying babies (see Appendix).

It's not unusual to feel inadequate, as if you are doing something wrong, when your baby continues to cry. But don't blame yourself or your baby – give yourself credit for coping, and give yourself a break whenever you can.

QUESTIONS AND ANSWERS

Q: How can I tell what my baby wants when she cries?

A: A new baby's cry doesn't vary much, but as she gradually learns that you come when she cries, it will become more as if she is calling you. Then you'll hear the difference if she gives a really frantic cry of urgent hunger or pain, or a grizzly, tired cry. There are other clues as well such as facial expressions, whether her body feels tense or relaxed, and how she is breathing. You will also have some idea of what she is crying for because you know what to expect from her own routine. As you tune into her you will be able to make a good guess about her message.

Q: Last night my baby wouldn't stop crying and I was so exhausted myself that suddenly I just couldn't stand it. If my husband hadn't been there I don't know what I would have done. Am I a terrible mother?

A: Because your baby's crying winds you up so powerfully, you may feel ready to snap when it doesn't stop. It's an unusual parent who never feels at breaking point, so don't blame yourself. What is important is recognizing the feeling and stopping before you lash out at your baby.

If you feel angry at your baby's crying it's time to put him down safely and take a break. You can't calm him when you are upset and angry yourself. If possible, hand over to a partner, ring a friend or go to a neighbour. If there is nobody you can go to, get away from your baby's crying until you calm down. Put on some music with headphones, have a bath with your ears under water,.

If you fear that you could hurt your baby, it's crucial that you tell your health visitor or doctor. You need help and support to deal with the strain and to arrange a safety valve for when everything feels too much.

Q: When my baby was little I never left her crying for long. But now she's 15 months old and she's started a whingey crying for attention. If I comfort her now when she cries, won't she make a habit of it?

A: As a baby gets older it is true that crying becomes less an automatic way of communicating needs, and sometimes can be a substitute for getting her message across by any other means. At 15 months, your daughter does need a lot of attention. Her own attention span is short, so she may get bored and need you to play with her and get her started on ideas with toys that she can then carry on with herself for a little while. The problem is not so much that she's asking for attention, as that the way she is asking is unpleasant.

It's still not a good idea to ignore her crying for long, because then when you do give her your attention she learns that if she just keeps it up long enough it will work eventually. Instead, you can try to take the focus off the crying and put it on to what her real message is. Don't offer cuddles and too much sympathy, but be more matter-of-fact and distract her from crying with interest in something else. Talk to her about what you and she are doing, put words to what you think she is asking and respond to other signals she gives. Then she will learn that crying is not the only way, nor the best way, to get your attention and that you both enjoy other ways of communicating more.

8

On to Solids

' At five months Karen decided she was ready to start solids. She'd been sitting on my lap while I had my meal, watching every bite from my plate to my mouth, when she finally grabbed some. So I gave her a nibble and she was away. It was really easy just beginning to let her have a bit of what we were having. '

TIME TO WEAN

Milk is the perfect food for your young baby, but eventually the breast or bottle is no longer enough and it is time for a gradual switch to eating and enjoying a wide range of foods. Though milk will continue to be your baby's main food and source of nourishment for some months after starting solid foods, various changes in your baby mark her readiness to move on.

Exactly when that point arrives is different from one baby to another, but generally between four and six months is the best time. At three months or before, your baby's system is not yet able to digest and absorb nutrients from food other than milk, and allergic reactions to foods given at this early stage are more likely. By four months and more your baby's gut has matured to be able to cope with solids, and allergies are not likely when foods are chosen and offered with care.

In the second half of the first year there are nutritional reasons why your baby needs solid food. Milk contains little iron, but your baby has prepared for this before birth by storing in her liver enough iron to last her through the first few months. But by around six months the iron stocks are beginning to run low and the iron provided by solid foods will be needed.

The way in which your baby is developing also gives you a clue that she is ready to start solids. She is able to sit up with support now and won't fall sideways. Teeth are beginning to emerge and even without back teeth your baby likes to gnaw and chew on things with her strong gums. By about six months she is able to use her tongue to move food to the back of her mouth, rather than automatically sticking her tongue out and pushing food out with it as she would before. And, very importantly, she is taking an active interest in everything and is likely to enjoy the new tastes and experiences of eating.

There are advantages in waiting until around six months to start solids if your baby shows no particular need or desire before then, because you skip the messy and time-consuming stage of feeding tiny amounts of nearly liquid food to a baby who spits most of it back at you. By about six months your baby is able to swallow more firmly textured food, can manage some finger foods and will move more quickly on to family food.

FIRST FOODS

There are many good possibilities for your baby's first food and since she will be taking only small amounts to begin with, the ease of preparation for you is almost as important as choosing an easily digestible food. A dry baby cereal which you can mix with a little breastmilk or formula is a good start – preferably rice cereal rather than wheat or oats, since rice contains no gluten which some babies are allergic to. Or you might prefer a cooked and puréed vegetable such as carrot, stewed and puréed apple or pear or mashed very ripe banana or avocado.

Food is fun, and by the time your baby is ready for solids he will be interested in new experiences of taste and texture. He also wants to be involved in the process of eating, so he can have a go with his own spoon long before he can manage it independently.

Whatever you decide on, it's wise to introduce only one food at a time, so you will know which food is a problem if your baby has any adverse reaction. Midday is a good time, since your baby will be alert and you will be able to keep an eye on her for the rest of the day. After two or three days of taking some of the first food, you can move on to include another.

Avoiding reactions

Some foods are more likely than others to disagree with your baby, either by causing an allergic reaction or by being difficult to digest. These foods are best left until your baby is about six months and happily taking other solids, and then introduced one at a time with a watchful eye for any reaction. Signs of your baby not being able to handle a food could be a rash, colic, vomiting, sore bottom, swelling of the lips, asthma or eczema. If any of these appear after introducing a new food, exclude it for a few weeks and then try it again.

The most common culprit foods include wheat products (unless they're gluten free), eggs, chocolate, citrus fruits, strawberries and mushrooms. Hard-boiled eggs can be an excellent source of important protein and minerals for your baby, but at first give her only the yolk, which is less likely to cause a reaction than egg white. If there is no problem with yolks you can later move on to egg white.

Commercial baby foods are very easy when you are away from home, and do not need to be heated if your baby likes them at room temperature. If you feed right from the jar, though, discard any leftovers.

COMMERCIAL OR HOMEMADE

There are advantages to both home-prepared and commercial baby foods, and many parents work out a combination of both to provide the best nourishment along with reasonable economy and convenience. When you prepare your baby's food yourself, you can use fresh ingredients that have maximum food value. Your baby gets used to home cooking right from the start, probably with a wider variety of tastes and textures than found in commercial food, and it can be easier to make the transition to family meals. It may be cheaper to make the food yourself, especially if you buy fruits and vegetables in season, and don't have to buy new equipment such as a blender to make purées.

The advantages of commercial baby food include convenience, and limiting waste by opening only small quantities at a time. Additives and preservatives are limited in baby foods and the ingredients are screened for pesticide levels. Read the labels so you know exactly what your baby is getting, remembering that they are listed in order of how much is present in the food. Single fruits and vegetables are better food value than mixed dinners, which may be mostly starchy cereal, and give you more control over introducing foods one at a time. No-sugar-added baby foods and drinks are available, but do check labels and beware of sugar listed under other names such as maltose, dextrose, glucose or fructose.

' I've started her at four months with gluten-free rusk mixed with banana, and she'll probably have that for a month or so before I give her a bit of baby rice in the morning. By about six months I think her daily routine will fit in with ours, so it will be easier for me than having different mealtimes. ' RACHEL

Sometimes adults are fooled into buying baby foods that sound good to adult tastes, but it makes much more sense to consider nutrition first and foremost. In any case, your baby is probably happier with simple flavours.

PREPARING EARLY MEALS

By the time your baby is ready for solids, it is no longer necessary to sterilize everything used in food preparation. Washing all utensils in hot water, as for the rest of the family, is enough. Basic food hygiene, such as washing your hands well before you begin and washing all fruits and vegetables before using, will help ensure safety. If you are using commercial baby food, don't feed directly from the jar or packet in case your baby eats only part and you want to save the rest in the refrigerator – instead spoon the part you expect him to eat into another dish.

Homemade food should be prepared without added salt because before the age of about eight months your baby's kidneys are not able to cope with excess salt. If you plan to use some of the food cooked for the family, cook without salt and let others add it at the table if they wish.

Initially food should be puréed in a blender or processor and then pushed through a sieve to make sure it is smooth, and any pips or tough skins should be removed from fruits or vegetables. First fruits such as apples, pears, peaches or apricots should be stewed in a little water before blending, but once cooked fruit is being eaten well you could serve fresh apple by scraping the sharp edge of a spoon across the apple flesh, until it is all scraped into a mush.

You may like to freeze food for your baby, since you will probably make more than he will want at one time. To minimize the risks of any bacteria, cool the cooked food quickly by putting it straight into the refrigerator, and then freeze as soon as it is chilled. Frozen fruits and vegetables need only be thawed thoroughly before serving and warmed if liked. Food containing meat or fish is less suitable for freezing, because it must be thoroughly reheated by boiling before it is safe to feed your baby, and in the quantities you will be using it is likely to stick to the saucepan and burn.

You can liquidize home-prepared food for your baby, and freeze some for later use. It works well to freeze the food in ice-cube trays, and then store the cubes in plastic bags in the freezer to later thaw or warm in baby-sized servings.

Early food should be fairly liquid, with added water or milk as needed, but as your baby becomes used to solids you can leave the texture a bit more firm and by six or seven months you can simply mash most vegetables rather than straining them.

After your baby is enjoying cereals, fruits and vegetables, you can move on to protein foods, such as cottage cheese, eggs, meat and fish. Meat and fish should be well cooked, blended and strained initially, but by about ten months meat can be chopped into tiny pieces and white fish can be flaked. Dry beans and lentils are high in protein, but to make them more digestible they must be soaked for several hours or overnight before cooking thoroughly.

FROM MUSH TO MEALS

Between four and six months, milk is still by far your baby's main source of nourishment, with solids perhaps boosting the range of nutrients, satisfying hunger and paving the way to broader eating habits later on. You will probably offer solids at one or two feeds each day, perhaps at midday and in the evening. Your baby will have more patience and interest in solid food if he is not too hungry, so you can take the edge off his hunger by giving him breast or bottle first, and interrupting the milk feed to have solids.

At six to eight months, your baby is branching out into more textures and tastes, but milk remains the centre of his diet. He is able to scoop up food with his hand to feed himself and can manage some finger foods, and may try to use a spoon.

Between eight and 12 months, your baby will probably have three solid meals a day. As the balance shifts so that solid foods form more of his diet than milk, you can start his meal with solids and then finish by offering him milk. He is now able to use his thumb and forefinger to pick up separate peas, and becomes adept at eating finger foods and fairly effective – though very messy – at using a spoon.

From one year to 18 months your baby is not growing as quickly as he did some months ago, and you may be surprised to find that he wants to eat less than he did before. Don't worry – as long as he is offered good wholesome food and not allowed too many biscuits or sweet drinks which fill him up between meals, he will eat what he needs for good growth and energy. By now he can fit fairly easily into family meals, and as long as everything is sufficiently chopped or cut he can largely feed himself. He will need help when he is tired, and may need reminding to eat when he is more interested in playing with his food than eating it. Use tact to support his efforts without taking over.

‘ Life seems a lot more set by routines now that he's having solid food and we have to get home for mealtimes or else cope with all the mess and palaver when we're out. Usually it doesn't seem worth it and we just aim to be home to fit his meal schedule. ’ SHEILA

Rusks, or the homemade equivalent – strips of bread slowly toasted in the oven until dry – are popular. Bread is more likely to break off and choke a young baby, but can be a good finger food by seven months or so. Chunks of cooked carrot or potato, cubes of cheese, pieces of banana, peeled orange segments or other soft fruits, can all be given by the age of six months.

SERVING BABY MEALS

You may like to hold your baby on your lap for the first few tastes of solid food, but before long it will be easier to put him in a seat. Be sure he is secured safely and that no hot food or drink is within his reach.

Messiness and baby meals go together, so to save on washing protect your baby's clothes with a bib. A soft plastic bib which includes sleeves is a useful item, or at least cover his front with a bib and push up his sleeves. Depending on your floor surface, you might also want to cover the floor around your baby's chair with newspapers, especially as he begins to take an active part in feeding himself.

You can use two spoons, one for you to feed your baby and one for him to hold. At first he will probably mostly wave it around, but before long he will be interested in putting it in his mouth. Before he is able to scoop food on to the spoon, you can fill the spoon and then swap with him so he begins to feed himself with the spoon. Though it is messy, the more you let him experiment and do as much as he can, the sooner he will eat independently.

As far as possible, you can feed your baby at the same time as the rest of the family. Meals are usually sociable times and he will more easily become a part of the family scene if he eats at the same times as others from early on.

Along with food in a dish, it's a good idea to serve some finger foods along with each meal. Finger foods allow your baby to be in charge of feeding himself and are usually keenly enjoyed. Never leave your baby alone with food. By ten months he will be able to eat raw apple, for instance, by gnawing on it with his gums, but front teeth may bite off a chunk which he could choke on. It's always essential to keep an eye on him.

DRINKS

As soon as your baby is taking much solid food, you should offer him some plain, cooled, boiled water to drink. He can begin to take drinks from a cup by five or six months. You may like to start him with a trainer cup with a spout, where the drinking action is somewhere between sucking and ordinary drinking. An advantage of trainer cups is that your baby can handle it by himself fairly soon, especially if you choose one with two handles (which can initially be one for you and one for him). It is perfectly possible, though, to go directly from breast or bottle on to taking some drinks from an ordinary cup. Skipping a trainer cup means your baby doesn't come to rely on the lid to prevent spills and may learn to use the ordinary cup on his own more quickly.

As solid meals increase, your baby will drop some milk feeds, but may have formula along with his meal (cow's milk contains too little iron and Vitamin D for babies under one year). By about ten months he may have a breastfeed or bottle just in the morning and before bed, with three solid meals in the day. For a breastfed baby the feed is as much about comfort as milk. For most babies the evening milk feed is the last to be dropped, and a breastfeed or bottle with the closeness and cuddling it brings can be enjoyed before bedtime well into or throughout the second year.

PREVENTING BECOMING OVERWEIGHT

In adult life obesity and being overweight contribute to some of the most prevalent and dangerous diseases, as well as causing a lot of personal unhappiness. Babies who are fat are more likely to become fat children and fat adults, partly because the fat storage cells which will be there for life are produced in

By 18 months your child can manage fairly independently with both eating and drinking. But he will still need tactful help when he is tired, off-colour, or distracted. He will also choose an overall good diet, as long as he is offered a range of wholesome foods.

FEEDING TIPS

- *Use a shallow, elongated weaning spoon with smooth edges for feeding your baby.*
- *Food can be served at room temperature, or slightly warmed.*
- *Never give your baby popcorn or peanuts, which are very dangerous if choked on and inhaled into the lungs.*
- *Start a pattern of healthy eating right from the start, with plenty of fruits and vegetables, and limiting sweet and fatty foods.*
- *Buy natural yogurt and add your own mashed or puréed fruit for better food value than sweetened fruit yogurts, which may also contain potentially harmful additives.*
- *Avoid food with additives. Some, especially colourings, are suspected of causing hyperactive behaviour in certain babies and children.*
- *Don't give your baby foods with small pips or seeds, such as raspberries or grapes, or granary bread with wheat kernels.*
- *Milk and plain water are the best drinks for your baby, with fruit juice occasionally. Sweet drinks can harm teeth even before they emerge, and coffee and tea are stimulants and block the uptake of some nutrients.*

the first year. Fat babies produce more of these fat cells which in later years are readily filled and swollen, so as adults it is easier for them to gain weight and harder to lose it. So preventing your baby becoming overweight can be a good protection for his future.

To prevent your baby becoming overweight, don't start solids too soon, and don't add sugar to your baby's food. Let him feed himself as far as possible, because then he will take what he needs rather than taking more because you are spooning it in and he enjoys the attention of being fed. He also won't be under pressure to have just a few more bites. Don't praise him for eating all his food, or show displeasure if he leaves something – to minimize waste, just give him small amounts at a time and provide more only if he has finished it and wants more.

Avoid the temptation to buy a few more minutes' peace and quiet when your baby fusses by handing him biscuits or sweets – besides being fattening, they are also bad for his teeth. Give him a bit of your time and attention instead and you won't be training him to reach for food whenever he feels a little unsettled.

There's no need, either, to think that handy snack food which your baby will enjoy needs to be 'junk' food with a lot of calories but not much else to offer nutritionally. Lots of nutritious foods like a banana, squares of wholemeal bread and butter, a piece of cheese or dried fruit are just as easy and popular with babies.

HAPPY MEALTIMES

Sharing a meal with others is a great pleasure for us sociable human beings, and your baby is no exception. He will enjoy your attention and involvement and be pleased to be part of a family scene when others are present. But with all this potential for mealtimes being the heart of family time together, there are few areas of family life which bring as much strife and worry – and problems often have their roots with the first solid meals.

Staying relaxed about what, how much, and how efficiently your baby eats leads to the most enjoyable family mealtimes. It also allows your baby to develop his natural healthy appetite without getting involved in a tangle of emotions.

Part of the trouble arises because we put a lot of emotional meaning into food. You can feel good inside when your baby eats and enjoys all the food you have carefully provided for him, but you may feel frustrated or even rejected if he turns away from it. So you coax him, urge him, spend extra time trying to sneak in one more mouthful, and he discovers that this is important to you and a sure way to get plenty of attention. The scene is set for a battle of wills that you can never win.

Stay relaxed about how much your baby eats and what he likes or rejects. A healthy baby will not starve himself and will eat what he needs if provided with a range of healthy food and left to get on with it. If you don't fill him up on biscuits and sweet drinks between meals through worry that he isn't eating enough, he will have a chance to get hungry between meals and will be sure to eat what he needs at mealtimes. He may have periods of refusing a food he loved the week before, or of passionate devotion to one particular food. Just let it pass, and he will be learning to rely on his healthy natural appetite – while mealtimes continue to be a happy time together.

QUESTIONS AND ANSWERS

Q: I'm concerned about my son having a good diet as well as protecting his teeth. Is it true that if a baby isn't given any foods with sugar added it will stop him developing a sweet tooth?

A: Babies have a natural attraction to sweetness – even breastmilk and bottle milk are quite sweet. So avoiding sugary foods won't stop your baby liking a sweet taste. But there is a difference between naturally sweet foods like fruits, which have a more subtle sweetness along with lots of other flavour, and the blast of pure sweetness from sugar. Refined sugar, unlike natural sweetness, also has a dramatic effect on blood sugar levels which leads to cravings for more. So avoiding added sugar is a good idea for your baby. As he gets older, you may find outlawing sweets and sugary foods is unrealistic, but you could compromise on limiting them to mealtimes and cleaning teeth afterwards.

Q: My daughter is nine months old and still isn't interested in solid food. I've gradually introduced her to a range of foods, but she will only eat a spoonful or two and then turns her face away. She seems happy just with breastmilk. Will she be missing out on what she needs?

A: Not all babies are eager to branch out into solid foods, and meanwhile breastmilk still provides a good nutritional base for your baby. Discuss with your health visitor, though, whether to give her a vitamin and mineral supplement with nutrients such as iron and vitamin D which are low in breastmilk. Continuing to offer solid food without any pressure will help your daughter to take pleasure in a wider range of food when she is ready. She may do well with finger foods to gnaw on and you could concentrate on iron-rich foods such as egg yolk, strips of wholemeal toast spread with nut butter, or cooked beans. Pieces of fruit contain vitamin C which helps iron to be absorbed better, too.

Q: I am vegetarian and would like to raise my baby to be vegetarian, too. Any pointers?

A: Your baby can flourish on a vegetarian diet, as long as you are careful to provide complete protein in non-meat foods. Vegetable proteins need to be combined to provide full usable protein, by serving pulses such as lentils or beans together with grains as in cereal, bread, pasta or rice. You can also combine grains with dairy products. Be sure the food is digestible for your baby by cooking it thoroughly and then grinding or sieving it to remove tough skins.

If you give your baby cheese, yogurt and eggs there should be no problem in providing complete nutrition, but there are different concerns if you decide on a vegan diet with no animal products. It is difficult to provide enough calcium in a vegan diet and almost impossible to provide vitamin B12 which is essential for the nervous system, so these should be supplemented.

Contact the Vegetarian and Vegan Societies (see Appendix) for further information on providing a healthy, balanced diet.

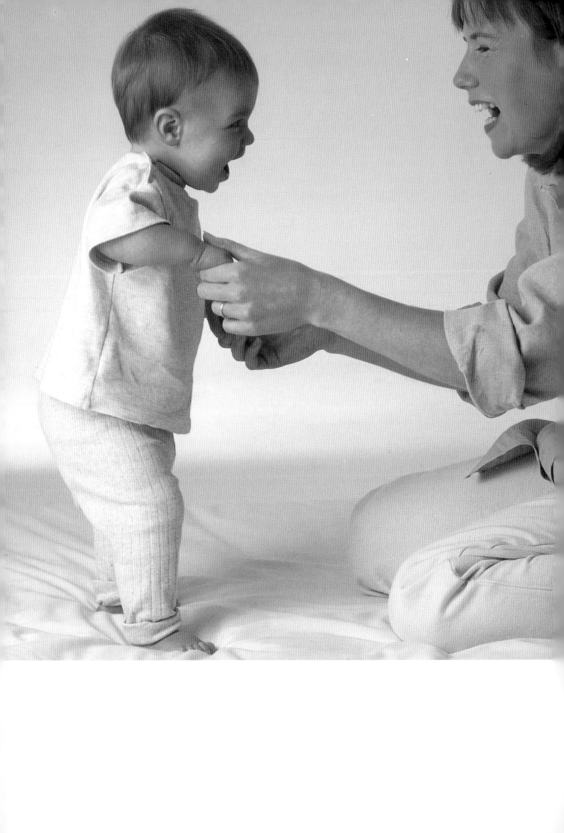

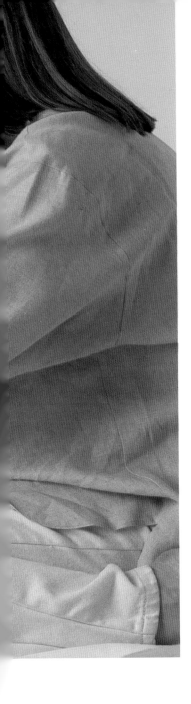

9

Growing and Changing

' When Peter was ten months old he discovered he could walk anywhere as long as someone held his hand. He became a little tyrant, pulling himself up on your leg and fussing until you took him for a walk, and he was so satisfied with that he refused to try walking alone for months. As soon as you let go of his hand, plop, he'd sit down on his bottom and complain loudly until someone agreed to take him walking again. '

FROM BABY TO TODDLER

In the first 18 months, your baby not only is growing faster than he will again in his whole life but also develops physical skills at an astonishing rate. Relying on his genetic makeup which programs him to grow into certain abilities, together with a lot of concentrated practice on his part, he develops from a helpless infant with very little control over his body to an upright, mobile little person who investigates the world around him with hands that push, pull, poke, squeeze and turn. Watching and encouraging your baby in his development is one of the greatest joys of being a parent.

GROWTH

Your baby's growth is fastest at birth and though the rate gradually drops he still grows quickly until about age three. He then enters the growth lull of childhood which lasts until the spurt at adolescence.

Just as babies are born at a range of birthweights and lengths, some babies continue to grow faster than others. In general, larger babies who are often destined to be larger adults gain both weight and height a little more quickly than smaller babies. On average, a baby will double his birthweight by about four to six months and triple it by one year, while length increases by about one quarter in the first year. But your baby is an individual and not an average, and it is impossible to predict exactly how fast your baby will grow.

After losing a few ounces right after birth, your baby will begin gaining weight which is likely to average around 150-175 g (5-6 oz) per week (see page 124). Weight gain probably won't be regular, though, and is more likely to appear as a series of gains and rests. Don't put too much importance on the week-to-week variations; as long as the overall pattern is one of fairly steady growth, a better guide to your baby's health is that he looks well, is alert, has plenty of energy and is interested and sociable with people around him.

As your baby grows, his body proportions change. His head which is relatively large at birth continues to grow rapidly through the first year, increasing in circumference twice as much as it will in the next 11 years. This reflects the brain growth which is crucial at the beginning of life. A young baby's legs are relatively short and insignificant, but gradually they grow longer and stronger. By the time a baby walks, he is less round tummy and more long legs.

‘ With your first you're desperate for her to do everything. I remember holding one hand behind Emma's back and saying, "Look, she can sit up". It's like a competition to see whose baby can do things first, which is ridiculous because they're all going to do things differently. ’ HELEN

As long as your baby is well nourished he will grow to reach his genetic potential. At times of illness growth may slow down, but a 'catch-up' period of faster growth afterwards means he won't be held back for long.

DEVELOPMENT

A measuring tape and scales can measure growth, but 'What is he doing now?' is the gauge of your baby's development. New activities and abilities – including tiny skills like holding his own hand as well as major milestones like sitting up, crawling and walking – appear one after the other, and your baby puts a lot of effort and attention into mastering them. The order of development is basically the same for every baby and proceeds from head to foot, and from the middle to the edges. So first your baby gains control of his eye and head movements, and arm control comes before leg control. He can make large movements with his whole arm from the shoulder before he can control the movements of his hand, and can use the whole hand before he masters individual finger movements.

Though every baby goes through the stages of development in roughly the same order, babies differ in how quickly they move through each stage, so all age guides to development are only approximate. Genetic inheritance plays a big part, by providing a blueprint for the whole process of maturing. Until a

A baby's head is big for his body, because of the early and rapid growth of the brain. As his nervous system matures he gradually gains control over his body, working down from head to arms and then to legs, and moving outward from trunk to limbs to fingers and toes.

GROWTH CHARTS

Whenever you visit the clinic your baby will be weighed and his/her weight will be plotted on growth charts similar to the ones shown below. Weight and height charts are designed to detect any problems with your child's physical development which might arise. The printed lines – (centiles) – show the upper and lower limits within which most children fall. Although it is interesting to know how your child compares with the 'national average', it is more important to show how your individual baby is faring, and health visitors will look for a steady rate of growth parallel to the centile lines on the chart.

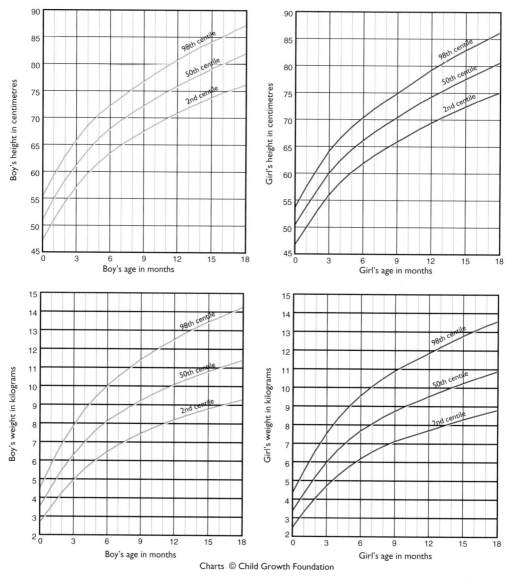

Charts © Child Growth Foundation

124

baby's nervous system, muscles and senses have matured to a certain point, he simply is not capable of particular skills, no matter how much practice and encouragement he is given. Rate of maturing tends to run in families, so there may be a family of early walkers or late walkers – neither of which will be better or worse at walking in the long run.

Your baby enjoys discovering new abilities and will love to practise them because they are innately satisfying. But she will also love it if you encourage her by showing you share her pleasure in the new activities.

How you encourage your baby in developing new skills does have an impact, too. It is true that if your baby has not matured to be ready for walking, for example, you cannot teach him to walk. But once he is ready, if you give him lots of opportunity to use his muscles, support when he needs it and show enthusiasm and praise for his efforts, he is likely to walk sooner than if you left him strapped in a pram for much of the day.

In all areas of development, you can help by providing a stimulating environment to capture his interest in reaching out and exploring. You also help by getting involved, playing and praising what he does, because he likes to please you. It's also important to know when to leave him to get on with things in his own way, since he knows best what he needs to master in order to move on. Sometimes there will be a studied look of concentration on your baby's face as he watches his own movements. When you see him concentrating on something don't distract him or overwhelm him with new ideas, but let him practise. He'll let you know when he's ready for something more.

Eyes and hands work together, as she learns to measure distance with her eyes, and to see what effect her reaching or swinging arms have on objects in space around her. Bright colours and interesting shapes attract her attention and encourage her to reach out and explore.

Head control

Birth: Your baby has little control over her heavy head, and needs you to support it in lifting and holding her.

One month: When lying on her tummy she can turn her head from side to side and lift it, but still needs her head and neck supported.

Two months: She can lift her head up and hold it briefly.

Three months: Her neck and upper back muscles have become strong enough so that when she is on her tummy she can lift and hold her head up as she props herself up on her forearms. When on her back, her head no longer lolls back as you lift her.

Five months: When she is on her back and you pick her up she lifts her head right up to help and has good strength in her neck, arms and upper body which may be enough for her to roll over.

Using hands

Discovering the connection between what our eyes see and what our hands can do is the key to much human activity, whether hammering, cooking, writing or drawing. For your baby the idea of space around her is an unknown, but once she learns to use her hands to find, feel and grasp the objects she sees, she has mastered a great tool to being active in the world.

Birth: Your baby has a grasp reflex which makes her fingers close on anything touching her palm. She will need to lose the reflex before she can learn to grasp things on purpose. Most of the time her hands are closed.

TIP: Put bright simple pictures and objects about 25 cm (10 in) away for her to look at. Learning to focus her vision and to be interested in things around her is the first step to reaching out to explore with her hands.

Two months: Your baby follows moving objects with her eyes and makes reaching movements with her whole arm as her hand opens and closes.

126

She may begin to watch her hands as she moves them around.

TIP: *Place a toy in your baby's hand so she can feel it and see it move as she moves her arm. A rattle lets her hear the effect of her movement.*

Three to four months: She discovers her hands, bringing them together and studying them. With jerky movements she will reach for objects, making a broad swipe with her whole arm and fist.

TIP: *Tie a length of elastic over her cot and dangle a toy from it just within her reach. Now and then add another toy, or fasten something new onto a familiar toy such as empty cotton reels, spoons and keys. Different shapes and textures are all interesting to her and those which make noises reward her for her efforts.*

Five months: As she reaches, she looks back and forth from the object to her hand to measure the distance. Now she can grasp an object, using her whole hand to grab it and usually bringing the other hand to hold it.

TIP: *Everything she grabs will go straight into her mouth for her to explore, so be sure there are no sharp edges and that no small objects which she could choke on are left in her reach.*

Six to seven months: She now reaches confidently, knowing just how far away something is. She can hold an object as if she were wearing a mitten, with her thumb away from the fingers; she may play with her toes.

TIP: *Hold toys out and let her take them from you. She will also enjoy watching you make toys work.*

With a strong back, coordinated arm movements, and confident reach and grasp, a baby can decide what he wants to do and then do it. Through experiences like this, he develops his own will and sense of being competent in the world around him.

Eight to nine months: Her grip is now less clumsy, as she holds an object between her thumb and the side of her index finger. She can take a toy from you and may hold it out to you, but still can't let go at will.

TIP: Continue to provide toys which will make a sound or movement, and which let your baby practise pulling, banging and rotating her wrist.

Ten to 12 months: She has learned to let go and loves to drop things over and over. She may throw things, can point and can pick up small objects by pinching them between thumb and index finger. She can post objects into holes and hold a crayon. She will enjoy 'pat-a-cake', clapping and may wave goodbye to people.

TIP: Play 'pick up' with her, retrieving the object she throws or drops time and again. Then try tying a toy onto her cot or chair with string so she can pull it back all by herself.

Thirteen to 15 months: She can hold two objects in the same hand and may pull off her socks.

TIP: Let her enjoy putting objects into a container one by one, by giving her a saucepan and lid with yogurt pots or anything else to put in, or a posting box toy.

Fifteen to 18 months: She can build a tower of three bricks, feed herself and scribble with pens or crayons.

TIP: Encourage her to feed herself, however messy, and play with her to give her ideas she can copy.

Sitting up

Being upright is stimulating to your baby because he can see more around him. Even in the first few weeks you can put him in an infant seat or car seat which will give firm support to his back in a slightly inclined position, and he will feel more a part of things going on around him. Later as he becomes stronger you can use a bouncer chair or prop him up in the corner of a sofa with cushions positioned for support. By holding him in a sitting position on your lap and giving him just as much support under the arms as he needs, you give him an opportunity to use the muscles that will help him to sit up.

Four months: Your baby's back is now strong enough for him to sit upright if well supported on the sides so he won't slip sideways. He can now enjoy the view if he sits in a baby backpack.

Six to seven months: He may sit alone for a few seconds, but still may lose his balance. In sitting alone he probably needs his hands on the floor for support. When propped with cushions, his hands are free for him to play.

Eight months: He now sits comfortably without support, but can't move much without falling over.

Nine months: Confident of his balance, he can lean over to reach something and come back to sitting, or twist around sideways. If you leave a selection of toys on the floor within his reach, he may use his broader range of movement to pick up and discard things as he plays.

A baby's personality and basic temperament can affect what skills he concentrates on. One baby may be adept at fine motor control and build a tower with ease while not yet walking, while another may not have time for such pursuits because he is eager to be up and away.

Crawling

Some babies never actually crawl but go straight on to pulling themselves up and walking, or they may develop another way of getting around such as scooting on their bottoms. Others are so pleased with the effectiveness of crawling that walking takes a low priority. Crawling styles vary too, from the classic forward movement to backward crawls, a kind of 'bear walk', or sideways crab steps.

Four months: When lying on his stomach, your baby will be able to lift himself up high taking his weight on his arms. He may also enjoy lifting both arms and legs and rocking on his stomach, as if he can't wait to take off.

Six months: He can now raise himself into a crawling position, and may rock back and forth on hands and knees.

Seven months: He begins to take his weight forward onto his arms and may pull a knee up underneath him.

TIP: You can encourage him to crawl when he's on the brink by offering him a toy that's just out of reach and praising his efforts to move toward it.

Eight to nine months: He's off! Once your baby is mobile be very careful about household safety (see page 184).

Walking – up and away

Most babies take their first independent steps – launching themselves into space with legs wide apart and elbows high – between nine and 15 months, after a lot of practice of standing and moving around with support. The normal age range is very wide, though, and some babies don't mature into walking until around 18 months.

Three months: If you hold your baby in a standing position on your knees as you talk to her, she will support some of her weight with her legs.

Six months: Held in a standing position, she now begins to bounce up and down. She may enjoy a bouncer to exercise her leg muscles.

Eight months: When held upright she can step with her feet, but her knees may sag under the weight after a while.

Bare feet indoors give better grip on the floor, and encourage healthy development of the feet through exercising the right muscles and distributing weight correctly. On cold floors, socks with grips on the bottom are the next best thing, with shoes reserved for outdoor excursions.

Nine months: She can pull herself up on furniture, but for a while she can't get back down again.

Ten to 12 months: With furniture for support, she begins to walk – first moving with her hands sliding along a surface and then moving from one support to another. As her skill and confidence grows, she will let go of a support and take one step to reach you. By one year, some babies will be taking a few independent steps.

'There was an awful moment when Imogen was six months and she got around by rolling. I'd gone out of the kitchen only for a minute and came back to find she'd rolled all the way across the floor and had her face in the dog's bowl and was eating the food. I rang the nurse and said, "What shall I do?" She said, "The dog eats the food and she's all right, isn't she? Well, she should be okay".' ANNE

Fifteen months: She still walks with feet wide apart and arms out for balance, but now she can stand up without support instead of pulling herself up. Once walking, she may not be able to stop without falling down.

Eighteen months: Her arms are closer to her sides now and she has much more control so she can stop or turn as she walks. She can bend down to pick something up and stand again, and can push or pull large toys.

TIPS: Bare feet indoors will help your baby to grip the floor and will help her foot muscles develop properly. If the floor is cold, a good alternative is soft socks with grips on the sole. Once your baby is walking by holding onto furniture, you could arrange some items to make the gaps small enough to reach between. Baby walkers give an opportunity to enjoy being upright and mobile, but won't speed up walking alone – they may even delay it by removing the incentive to try walking unaided.

IS SOMETHING WRONG?

Most parents watch eagerly for their baby to reach the next milestone and may begin to feel anxious if their baby seems to lag weeks behind others in particular skills. It may be difficult not to compare your baby with others. But keep in mind that babies differ widely in their inborn rate of developing, as well as their personalities which can make one baby eager and active physically while another is more interested in babbling and learning to talk.

If you are worried about your baby's development, discuss your concern with your doctor who will probably put your mind at rest, but can arrange for more thorough assessment if necessary. Since you know your baby best, your feeling that something is wrong can be an important indicator that careful checks are needed.

Some problems which can cause disability are apparent at birth, but others may show up only gradually as the weeks and months pass and the baby does not follow the normal sequence of development. Perhaps the baby is floppy and does not develop muscle tone to control his head or sit up, or perhaps visual problems interfere with reaching and grasping. The earlier problems like this are identified, the sooner appropriate help can be given.

With love and attention to particular needs, both to physical and mental stimulation, a child with Down's syndrome can develop into an active and positive member of a family, and eventually of society. Parents often say that though the demands of them are great, they are amply rewarded by the child's joy and affection.

When it is discovered that a baby has a disability, there is profound shock and grief for the parents who may feel as if they have lost their perfect child. At the same time, when a disability is discovered some time after birth the baby is already loved and accepted as an individual. The family can be helped to deal with the tragic blow by the health service, which should provide counselling as well as clear guidance and instruction in caring for the child. Contacting other parents with similar experience is also a help in sharing anxieties and fears for the future and providing practical advice and help.

The baby is already learning to cope with the abilities he has and is not aware of a problem. Parents should be given a prediction which is as accurate as possible of the effects of their baby's problem. But the effect on a baby depends partly on the help he receives to live with his disability. The extra care and attention the baby requires can put enormous strain on a whole family far into the foreseeable future, without the usual rewards parents expect from their developing child. On the other hand, a different degree of giving can result in a different degree of reward, as every small advance is a triumph. Some families have found the experience of having a child with a disability draws them closer together, and responding to the challenge can bring them a richer outlook on life.

PHYSICAL MILESTONES

What baby can do	Approximate age
Roll over, front to back	4-6 months
Roll over, back to front	5-7 months
Sit without support	6-9 months
Crawl	9-11 months
Walk with support	10-12 months
Walk alone	13-18 months

TEETH

All of your baby's first teeth are in the jaws before birth, and the permanent teeth have even started to form. Just when they begin to appear is governed by genes and nothing in diet or habits will have much effect on when teething begins. Diet does have a large influence, though, on the strength and health of the teeth, starting with a good calcium-rich diet for the mother during pregnancy, and right through childhood for your baby.

Rarely has a baby a tooth already present at birth, while at the other extreme it can be a year before teething begins. Most babies, however, cut their first tooth around four to six months of age.

Some babies give no notice of teething and you might simply find one day that a tooth has appeared. Or you may notice a light bulge on the gum or red patch on the gum and cheek, followed in a day or two by a tooth. Other babies have much more discomfort with teething and may be grizzly and irritable, waking in the night, dribbling more than usual, or crying during feeding or if a spoon hits the sore spot on the gum.

Order of teething

The order in which teeth appear is the same for almost all babies, even though the timing differs. The first teeth to appear are the central bottom pair of incisors, on average at four to six months. These are followed by the two central top incisors, and then the top teeth either side of those. Then the next bottom incisors appear, so that by about one year the average baby will have all four central cutting teeth top and bottom.

A gap then appears as the lower and upper molars, grinding teeth further back in the mouth, arrive at around 12 to 14 months. The gap is filled in by the pointed canine teeth which appear starting at around 18 months. The set of first teeth will only be complete when the second set of molars appear at the back at around age six (see page 134).

Caring for teeth

Though your baby's first teeth will be replaced later in childhood by the permanent teeth, they are still of great importance. Not only are they needed through childhood for eating and good appearance, but they maintain the correct positions to guide the permanent teeth into place. Good habits of caring for teeth started in babyhood can last your child a lifetime.

A good diet will help keep teeth and gums healthy by providing the right nutrients for growth. There may be fluoride added to the water supply in your area, which also helps form strong tooth enamel – check with your health visitor about fluoride in your area.

You can also prevent tooth decay by avoiding some foods. Decay occurs when bacteria feeding on a sticky coating of plaque on the teeth secrete acid which eats into the teeth. So avoiding the formation of plaque can protect teeth. Sticky sweets and sugared foods, including drinks, are the worst offenders in forming plaque, while raw fruit and vegetables help to clean the teeth. If you do give your baby sweets or puddings, try to keep them to mealtimes when you can clean the teeth or at least rinse with water afterwards, rather than between meals when the sugar may stay on the teeth for hours.

Your baby's teeth and gums should be cleaned regularly as soon as teething begins. Wiping the gums will help remove the milky residue which could stick to teeth as they emerge. Wet a small gauze square and use it to rub your baby's teeth and gums once or preferably twice a day. As she approaches one year give her a baby toothbrush and let her copy you as you brush your teeth. You will still need to clean her teeth for her until she is about three years old, but she will be developing the idea of routine care for her teeth.

Easing teething discomfort

Most teething gels for numbing sore gums aren't recommended because your baby then swallows the medicine, and over the course of all the teething he will do in the first year that would amount to quite a lot. Cold is soothing, so you could give him a fluid-filled teether cooled in the refrigerator – but not the freezer, which could cause frostbite. A carrot is good for him to gnaw on, or you could rub his gum with your finger. If he is very fretful in the night you could give him one dose of paracetamol to help him sleep, but again don't make a habit of it. Homeopathic Camomilla can be helpful. Be sure not to put signs of illness down to teething. Fever, vomiting, diarrhoea or signs of a cold do not come from teething, so see your GP about any of these symptoms.

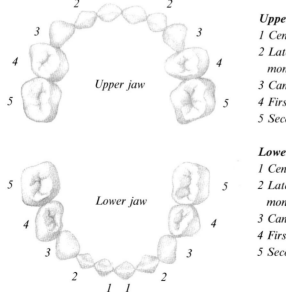

Upper jaw
1 Central incisors 6-8 months
2 Lateral incisors 8-10 months
3 Canines 18 months
4 First molars 12-14 months
5 Second molars 6 years

Lower jaw
1 Central incisors 4-6 months
2 Lateral incisors 10-12 months
3 Canines 18 months
4 First molars 12-14 months
5 Second molars 6 years

QUESTIONS AND ANSWERS

Q: How soon can I tell if my baby will be left-handed or right-handed?

A: Signs of a preference for one hand or the other may appear from the very start, in which way your baby usually turns his head when lying down. Once he starts to reach for things he may show a preference, tending to reach first with one hand in particular. Some babies seem to have a definite one-sided dominance early on and stick to it, but most use either hand equally until they are about one year old. Even after that, small children may change hands for different tasks and not show a clear dominance of one hand over the other, while a few remain ambidextrous, using either hand equally.

Q: Over a month ago my little girl took a few steps on her own, but she seems to have forgotten all about it and now she just crawls. Is this normal?

A: Developing new skills doesn't go steadily, but rather in fits and starts. It is normal for a baby to have a spurt and do something new and then just continue practising until she has mastered it without going on to the next step, or leave it while she concentrates on something else. Your daughter won't have forgotten how to walk, but she may have put it on a back burner while she tries out a few words. When she's ready she'll probably surprise you by suddenly taking off on two feet.

Q: Now that my baby is crawling I use a stair gate, but she is fascinated with the stairs and always makes a beeline for them. When can she learn about stairs?

A: Babies do like to climb, so she is capable of going up stairs soon after she can crawl. It's a good idea to teach her now, in case she does ever find stairs unguarded. Let her crawl up, with you behind her – and if you ever discover her going up don't call and distract her which could cause a fall, but just quietly get behind her. With you below her on the stairs, show her how to go down by crawling backwards. She will continue to crawl up and down stairs for some time after she can walk, but between 18 months and two years will begin to walk up and down stairs.

Q: Should I give my baby fluoride drops to protect her teeth?

A: Fluoride does have a significant effect in helping to prevent tooth decay by making the tooth enamel harder. In some areas the water supply contains fluoride, while in others children can receive fluoride drops or chewable tablets. Check with your health visitor about the situation in your water authority, and whether she recommends fluoride supplements for your baby.

10

Learning

'I'm just stunned at how much he's learned in a few short months. He picks things up so fast and you can almost see the wheels turning as he puts two and two together. Sometimes when he doesn't want to go to sleep it seems he's just too busy finding out about things to bother with sleep.'

EMERGING FROM THE SENSUAL WORLD

Think of a dream – where something may appear one minute and disappear the next, a person may somehow become a tree or turn into someone else the next time you look, you may float through space or fall without ever reaching the ground. You don't know why or how things happen here and though you may shake your head in puzzlement when you wake up, it all seemed perfectly acceptable at the time. You weren't applying the rules of logic, but just taking it all as it came.

To a new baby, life may be something like this – but even more so. With no knowledge of the past or idea of the future, a baby receives a wealth of impressions through her senses. Light, colours, sounds, smells, tastes and contact through touch come and go. She doesn't know what causes them. She doesn't even know that she is a separate being and that her own waving hand belongs to her any more than your face which appears before her.

But from the very beginning, she is intelligent. Though she has everything to learn, she begins right from the start to store her impressions and gradually make sense of the world around her. Human babies have the longest period of development of all animals, because instead of behaving mostly from instinct, human brainpower allows us to reason, to predict and solve problems – and we need time for all that learning.

PARENTS AS TEACHERS

In many ways, you are the most important teachers your baby will ever have. You help to set the right conditions for her natural curiosity and intelligence to blossom, and for her to learn *how* to learn. You give her the confidence and will to reach out, take a chance, experiment and discover.

Security

By loving your baby and caring for her, you give her the basic security of knowing that she will be looked after. In learning to trust that she will be safe and her needs will be met, she develops the confidence to try something new. As she grows she will be eager to explore and experiment, as long as you are nearby for her to run back to whenever she needs your reassurance.

Though her growing trust in life and in you is essential for her to reach her full potential, this doesn't mean that she always has to be happy and you must instantly solve all her problems. Life isn't like that – sometimes immediate help isn't possible and there are no magic solutions to some problems. Being 'good enough' parents means meeting her needs most of the time. In fact, part of a healthy sense of security involves learning that it's not the end of the world to feel unhappy or to fail at something. If she trusts the loving care behind her, she can learn to take the bumps and hurdles in her stride and have another go.

Stimulation

By providing stimulating surroundings, you introduce your baby to the world. You give her things to look at and touch, play with and listen to. In everyday activities you talk to her, helping her to notice and respond to things around her. Be careful, though, not to overload her with too much stimulation. She can concentrate better on one thing at a time and surroundings with too much constant noise and activity will interfere with her efforts to make sense of things. Give her the opportunity to learn how to direct her attention for herself, choosing what to concentrate on from among all the possibilities around her.

Responding

The best education always starts where the learner is and takes them one step further. Nobody can help your baby learn better than you, because you know her best and can respond to her signals. You are aware of what she is interested in and what she is trying to do, so you can repeat for her the activity she is concentrating on. When she's had enough of that, you can vary it just slightly to give her a new experience to expand her range of understanding. Your response increases her interest, too, because she loves your involvement.

Safety

Safe surroundings are important for your baby's learning. By providing safe bounds, you make it possible for her to explore without the constant interruption of being told 'no' – so she is more confident and curious and you are more relaxed and supportive. (See page 165 on Safety Tips for Toys, and pages 183-4 on Accident Prevention and Safety in the Home.)

You are your baby's first teacher, and the experience you build now in doing things together is the foundation of her education for life. Even once a child is learning in school, the involvement with parents at home is one of the biggest factors in her continued learning.

Help

By being a partner in your baby's activities and offering a helping hand when what she wants to do is beyond her abilities, you expand her experience and cut down on frustration. For instance, maybe she wants to build a tower of three bricks so she can then knock them down again, but it keeps falling over as she tries to put on the top brick. Your tactful help of holding the bottom bricks steady as she places the third will allow her to complete the process – which she may want to repeat over and over to make sure that hitting them with her hand always has the same effect.

HOW BABIES LEARN

Psychologists study the way babies learn and how they develop understanding of the world by watching babies' reactions to things. Of course they can't discover just what a baby is thinking, but they can make educated guesses based on how he behaves. It may be which picture a baby looks at longest, or whether his heartrate speeds up with excitement when something happens.

You might enjoy observing your baby's growing understanding, by watching how he reacts at different ages. If you move a toy across his vision, does he follow it with his eyes? If it disappears from his view, does he seem surprised when it reappears, or as if he expected it? Once he can sit up, you can show him a toy and then hide it under a cloth. At what age does he lift the cloth to look for it? When does he begin to predict based on past experience, so he seems to know getting the backpack means you are going out?

Taking your baby out is an enjoyable experience which gives him the chance to learn about his environment. Most babies enjoy the change of scene, fresh air and new sights and sounds. A very young baby can be taken out in a pram or a sling and the rhythmic movement is likely to send him to sleep. By about four months he may prefer a forward-facing pushchair or baby backpack which give him a better view.

The senses

Babies gather information about the world through the five senses, often concentrating seriously on what they can see and hear. The most interesting sight for a baby is a human face, but your baby will also be interested in simple patterns in strong colours. A baby stores the sensory impressions in his memory, soon beginning to recognize familiar images. He shows more interest in something slightly different from the familiar, rather than something totally new.

' Once when Matthew was only a few weeks old I'd cut out some pictures from bright-coloured pieces of felt and glued them on to his cot bumper. The first time he saw them as I laid him in his cot at night it was like he'd had an electric jolt, he was so excited. He cried when I turned the light off and I had to leave it on for him to lie there studying the shapes and colours. ' JANE

Experimenting and practising

Just like a scientist, your baby begins by observing the world around him and he soon begins to sort out his impressions into patterns. He notices that certain things go together, so for instance when he hears your voice he expects you soon to appear, which he may associate with contact and food.

He begins to predict things and wants to test whether his predictions are right. If he swings his arm and it hits the hanging rattle, will it always move and make a sound? When he sits in his highchair and lets go of a toy, will it always fall to the floor? In the bath, when he slaps down his arms, will water fly? Later, when he reaches for a stream of running water, why can't he grab and hold it? With each new understanding, he must test what happens over and over until he is sure he has got it right.

Imitation

Your baby also learns by copying you. At first he imitates by instinct, copying your facial expressions without knowing he is doing it. But gradually it comes more under his control, and through imitating your actions, sounds and expressions, he tries out many skills. He cannot copy something too different from what he can already do, but if you start by copying his sounds and gestures he becomes more aware of them and then can go on to imitate variations you add on. As he grows older he will continue to mimic your actions and you may be surprised at how detailed his observations of you were.

Emotions

Along with copying your behaviour, your baby is very sensitive to your feelings and copies them, too. If you meet new situations with a positive outlook and confidence, your baby will feel confident, too. But if you react with fear and anxiety, your baby will pick that up and tend to withdraw from unfamiliar situations. So to encourage curiosity and learning, show feelings of pleasure in new discoveries and share them with your baby.

DEVELOPING UNDERSTANDING

Birth to four months: When just a few days old, babies show they can recognize their mothers' voice and smell. Your baby's visual focus is short at first, but she will follow your face with her eyes if you are close enough. Within a few weeks she will recognize your face. Bold simple patterns capture her interest first and as her focus expands she will be interested in looking at objects with texture and three dimensions, rather than flat, smooth objects.

By three to four months, she can remember other people and events in her daily routine, such as her feeds, baths and toys. She will laugh and coo with pleasure at familiar things and may not be happy with changes in her routine and caretaker.

Five to six months: Your baby becomes very interested in shaking and pulling and making things happen. She is also more aware of detail now and so may become attached to a particular toy. She doesn't think objects out of her view no longer exist, but her attention span is too short for her to look for them. If you partly cover a toy with a cloth, she will pull it out, but if it is totally covered she forgets about it and doesn't search – it's a matter of 'out of sight, out of mind'.

Eight to ten months: Your baby is establishing an idea of herself as a separate person and begins to show a will of her own. She recognizes her own name and quite a few other words. She also recognizes objects and people when she sees them in unfamiliar situations. Instead of investigating most objects by feeling them in her mouth, she uses her hands and eyes to study things. She will now look under a cloth to find a hidden toy.

Twelve to 18 months: At this age your baby loves to get a reaction from you and will repeat again and again something that makes you laugh – or even angry. She wants to experiment with everything, including her food at mealtimes and water in the bath. Her attention span has grown, so she can concentrate by herself for quite a while. She understands that flat pictures in a book stand for real objects and she can think of something she can't see and name it. She can invent solutions to problems and may use a tool to reach something, or move a box to climb up on. She imitates actions not only when she sees them, but later in the day or days later. She also begins to imagine and pretend, making an animal sound for a toy animal, or crashing cars together. She can follow simple instructions.

WHO AM I?

One of the important things your baby learns is that he or she is a separate individual, acting in the world and affecting other people and things. This is the beginning of the self-concept, which will be developed and altered throughout life by comparison with others, self-knowledge and what others say. A realistic self-concept helps in choosing appropriate goals and activities.

But there is a danger in a self-concept being too limiting to let a person reach his full potential, turning away from positive experiences or opportunities because 'it's not me'.

Even in the first year your baby is forming his self-concept in a way which may set a pattern for life. Some of his ideas of what he is like as an individual come from your reactions to him, what you encourage in him and what you say about him. Babies do have individual personalities right from the start, but be careful not to try to pin your baby's character down and put a label on it.

The basis of your baby's self-esteem – feeling good about himself and liking the person he is – lies in the love he receives. Because you love him, he knows he is lovable. Whatever else he happens to discover about his individual personality, deep down he feels secure and happy in himself.

If parents see their baby as 'boisterous and adventurous' they may provide lots of active things to do – but may neglect seeing his quiet, thoughtful side and giving him opportunities to develop that. Or perhaps they consider him 'shy and timid'; it may be that he needs to observe a situation for a while before he's comfortable in exploring it, but with patient support and encouragement he may enjoy venturing forth and become more bold. Especially if you have more than one child there may be a tendency to compare them and note their differences, but be careful not to push them into boxes which describe them. Labels are limits, and children usually grow to fit them. What a baby needs instead is respect for his own temperament, along with an open-ended encouragement to develop his potential in every sphere.

Girl or boy?

Gone are the days when society as a whole held rigid ideas of what sort of toys and actitivites, and later what sort of role in life, were appropriate for each sex. But the more subtle assumptions which can colour a baby's self-concept and learning remain. It is true that there are a few differences between the behaviour and skills of girls and boys. For instance, girls on average learn to talk earlier and do better at early reading. It could be, though, that these differences are totally the result of boys and girls having been treated differently from babyhood. Studies have shown that people tend to talk more and make more eye contact with baby girls, so it's not surprising that they are faster at language and communication skills. On the other hand, they tend to give baby boys more active toys and praise physical skills.

Whatever natural differences in learning there may be between males and females, what is certain is that individual differences are wider and more important than those between the sexes. So rather than limiting your baby by encouraging either a boyish or girlish side, follow his or her lead in interests and activities to develop all your baby's qualities.

A MIND OF HIS OWN

From just accepting everything as it comes, your baby gradually learns to control his actions and realizes that his actions can have an effect. Now he has his own ideas and develops a will to back them up.

These first stirrings of independence add a new dimension to your relationship, and it begins to be more two-way rather than all the ideas and decisions coming from you. Inevitably, there will be times of conflict when you don't accept what he wants to do, and the need for discipline arises.

Conflict

Why might you object to your baby's behaviour? A very important reason, and one where you may have little room for compromise, is danger. Baby-proofing your home will help minimize the number of times safety concerns mean you must stop your baby exploring. Nevertheless, there is always something your baby can climb on or into or grab which poses a danger, and which you must stop. On the other hand, it is possible to be over-protective, stopping your baby from challenges which may prevent his learning and mastering new skills. Sometimes you could let him try what he wants to do, with

‘ I feel like a policeman all day long, saying "Don't touch this, don't touch that". We've moved all the breakable things away, but it's things like the stereo, opening doors; and the plants are very popular, too. I can say 'no', but I don't think he remembers from one minute to the next what I don't want him to do. He doesn't play with the things I put out for him. For peace, I take him for long walks in the pushchair and he loves that. ’ SALLY

TEACHING YOUR BABY

◆ *If you hang up a mobile toy for your baby, alter just one thing at a time for greatest interest.*

◆ *Let your baby learn about all sorts of materials, not just smooth bright plastic toys. Give objects made of wood, metal, cloth of different textures and crinkly paper.*

◆ *A young baby's senses are easily overloaded, so avoid a hectic atmosphere and constant background noise.*

◆ *Put different substances, such as perfume, vinegar, lemon juice, vanilla, on balls of cotton wool and hold them for your baby to smell.*

◆ *Play 'peek-a-boo' with your baby – it's fun as well as showing that you haven't really disappeared just because you are covered up.*

◆ *Start maths concepts by talking about things being empty, full, big, little, 'one' and 'two' objects.*

◆ *See if your baby can begin to sort objects – clothes pegs in one pan and spoons in another, or sort by colour.*

◆ *Taking time over ordinary routines and talking about them will provide fertile ground for learning.*

◆ *Rely on your baby's natural curiosity for learning rather than trying to programme specific ideas, and above all let it all be fun.*

---

your careful supervision. You will need to use your judgement and knowledge of your baby's capabilities to decide how much you can allow.

Or you might want to stop some behaviour because it makes too much mess and work for you. Maybe he wants to learn about vaseline by shoving his hand in the jar and grabbing the contents, or he wants to pull all the pans and lids on to the kitchen floor for the sixth time in an afternoon. But you do not want the consequences of clearing it up.

Sometimes you might be in too much of a hurry to let him do things in his own way. When you are in a rush to get home and make dinner you may not be able to let him toddle behind the supermarket trolley 'helping' you push it, but instead want to pop him into the seat for a quick whip round.

Distracting

When you must stop your baby's behaviour for whatever reason, the most successful tactic is to distract his attention on to something else. If he has grabbed something dangerous, take it away with one hand while you offer an alternative with the other. Talk to him about what you are offering as a distraction, and it will usually be readily accepted. By spotting signs of trouble coming and using distraction early on before he gets too set on what he wants to do, you can steer clear of most head-on conflicts.

Saying 'no'

Sometimes a quick response is needed – for instance, in avoiding immediate danger – and other times distraction may not be successful. At these times you will have to say 'no' to your baby, as you physically prevent the unacceptable behaviour by taking something away or moving your baby. By about eight months your baby can understand what 'no' means, and if you save it for times when it is really necessary it can have a strong impact.

There is no need to accompany 'no' with a shout and a baby should never be smacked, which will frighten and confuse him. Your firm tone of voice, the expression on your face and your determined manner will convince him.

Your baby wants your attention and your approval. If he is trying to get a reaction by doing something you have said 'no' to, don't accidentally reward him with your attention by making a big fuss. Remove the source of the trouble, or him from the scene if necessary, with little comment. Then give him plenty of hugs and smiles when he is doing something you approve of.

Never naughty

When a baby pulls the cat's tail, knocks over your best lamp, or spills his milk on the floor, he is not being naughty. He just doesn't understand about someone else feeling pain or caring about a lamp or a mess on the floor. So stop him in what he's doing if necessary, and let him know that you dislike his behaviour – tell him it hurts, or it's a nuisance. But don't say he is 'bad' for doing it. He needs to know that you still love him and approve of him even when you don't like what he does, and that you will teach him what you expect of him.

When you need to stop your baby doing something, remember that she doesn't know any better. By teaching her patiently and with respect for her feelings, and letting her know why her behaviour isn't acceptable, you are helping her gradually develop the ability to temper what she wants with the needs and feelings of others.

QUESTIONS AND ANSWERS

Q: Can my baby learn by watching television?

A: Television has little to offer a baby. It may surround the baby with the rhythm and sounds of language, but she can't pick out separate words. It is no substitute for real interactions and conversations based on what she can really see and feel. Because television offers so little, most babies aren't interested anyway – and having it on much of the time can teach them to tune things out rather than be alert and interested.

Q: At 12 months my baby always plays with his food and it ends up everywhere. Should I stop him and try to start teaching him table manners?

A: A one-year-old does learn by exploring his food, feeling it and seeing what it will do as well as eating it. At some point, though, he crosses the line between learning as part of eating and simple playing. You naturally object to unnecessary cleaning up, and learning table manners is really about respecting how others feel. So if you feel he is not really studying his food, but just enjoying smearing or throwing it, do put a stop to it. Just get him down with little comment, and he'll soon learn where you draw the line.

Q: When I take my baby daughter to mother-baby group, the other babies crawl around but she is timid and clingy. Will she be behind the others because she doesn't get on and do things?

A: Being bold and exploring new surroundings is a good way for babies to learn, but it can only come when a baby is ready. Trying to force independence too soon can prolong the clinginess, because it can frighten a baby and make her feel less confident. Try sitting down on the floor with your baby and let her investigate things from a feeling of safety near you. Don't worry about her learning since it goes in spurts and she can discover a lot in a short time when the right time comes.

Q: At what age do babies learn to play together, and do they need contact with other babies to learn to be sociable?

A: Most babies seem to enjoy having other children around and by the time they are a few months old they are aware of other babies. At a year or so they may enjoy playing alongside another baby and may copy each other, but won't really cooperate and play together for another year. In the meantime, your baby is learning to be sociable from being with you.

Q: My baby is becoming very willful about little things like not sitting in his chair when his meal is ready. Should I insist so he learns to behave?

A: The beginnings of good discipline lie in respecting other people's feelings, and one way to teach that to your baby is to show respect for him. When he's playing and it's time for a meal, you needn't whisk him away, but tell him and gain his cooperation. Let him make choices such as to wear his boots around the house, and let him feel important by helping you put the carrots in the pan for dinner. He imitates you in most things including attitude and if you are considerate of him he will learn to be considerate too.

11

First Words

‘ She didn't say a single word until she was nearly two years old, and sometimes I wondered if she was ever going to say anything at all. But just listen to her talking now! Even before she spoke, she always managed to make herself understood. ’

NATURAL ABILITY

A long cosy chat, a whispered secret, a joke, an explanation – no wonder the prospect of your baby beginning to speak holds such promise. Your communication is enriched and you can learn directly what your baby thinks once he begins to develop the wonderful gift of speech. Using language well is also an important key to effective learning throughout life.

Learning to talk does come naturally and at times it seems that a baby effortlessly soaks it up like a sponge, unlike the effort spent by an adult trying to learn a foreign language. But though babies are born with the ability to learn to speak, language skills are not automatic and must be learned. Throughout the first year of life and beyond, your baby is learning the basic skills which prepare him for those momentous first purposeful words.

Telling you something in words is a long way from his first days where crying was his only means of communicating a need. A newborn baby's vocal cords are like a hollow tube and his throat and tongue must mature before he can learn to make and control a range of sounds. He must also be able to hear the sounds he makes and compare it with other sounds around him. He has to understand that a particular sound stands for a particular thing or idea – that words have meaning. And he must be motivated to want to tell you something. You have an important role to play in helping your baby prepare for talking in all these ways.

ON TO TALKING

In the first month your baby is already developing his lips, tongue and vocal cords as he feeds, sucks his fist and makes small noises, usually 'uh' sounds from the back of his throat. He listens to human speech with more interest than any other sound. In fact, he begins to pick up the rhythm of language by making tiny movements with his whole body in time with speech. He will also watch you, especially your mouth, as you speak to him.

At six weeks your baby responds to a voice by smiling, and when he looks at you he may open and close his mouth as though he were trying to talk. He may also have begun to have 'conversations', taking turns with you as he gurgles, waits for your reply and then gurgles again.

By three months your baby enjoys making cooing sounds, 'aah' or 'oo', and will happily entertain himself with the sounds. A special trigger which makes him coo even more is having someone's attention, which he notices when you make eye contact with him. He will start 'conversations' now and watch your mouth intently when you respond to him.

' A lot of people say their baby's first word is "Dada", or maybe "Mama". But Stephen's was "backpack". He loved going out for a walk in the baby backpack, and whenever he'd see us take it down from the rack he'd reach for it and say "backpack, backpack" until he was in it and on his way. ' SHEILA

150

It's fun to play with sounds, and a baby may lie in her cot babbling happily to herself. But making sounds and responding to different sounds we hear is also part of being sociable, and your baby will be alert to the sounds you make and enjoy having chatty, babbling 'conversations' with you.

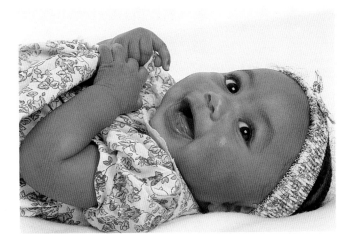

At five to six months your baby's vocal muscles are more like an adult's and he has more control over his lips. Now he can make consonant sounds, and babbles syllables such as 'da', 'ma', 'pa'. He may spend less time vocalizing than at three months, but the sound is beginning to be like his native language as he learns how to make the sounds spoken around him and uses the rhythms and ups and downs in his voice. He will enjoy chatting with you and will listen and try to imitate a sound you repeat several times for him.

At eight months your baby is very aware of adult conversations and will watch in turn the person who is speaking. He may shout and sometimes his babbling may be quite musical.

At nine to ten months his babbling is strung together to sound just like sentences and he will enjoy you answering him in real sentences of similar length. He babbles alone, or in conversation. He can understand quite a few words and will be able to respond with appropriate actions when you tell him or ask him something – he may point when you ask 'Where's Mummy's nose?'

Between ten and 12 months your baby may well say his first word. The first word grows out of using sounds and gestures to communicate to you, and sometimes it may be almost accidental that he makes a sound you recognize as a word. Your enthusiastic response urges him to keep trying. Though he may not have the sounds exactly right, he does intend you to understand what he means and he will be delighted when you do.

From 12 to 15 months new words are slowly added to your baby's vocabulary, maybe one or two a week. He may seem to forget about talking temporarily while he is busy learning to walk. Most of his words are the names of things and mimicking animal sounds may be favourites. He may include some action words like 'look' or 'go', describing words like 'pretty' or 'hot', or social words such as 'bye-bye'. If he says two words, it is because he always hears them together and thinks of them as one word, such as 'all gone'.

ENCOURAGING BABBLING

◆ *Give your baby your undivided attention and return his smiles.*

◆ *Talk to your baby in short sentences and wait for a reply.*

◆ *Copy the sounds your baby makes.*

◆ *Change the sound a little ('la' instead of 'da') and see if your baby can copy you.*

◆ *Limit background noise so your baby learns to listen more carefully.*

◆ *Sing and hum to your baby and tell her nursery rhymes.*

◆ *Talk about your everyday routines so your baby can enjoy the rhythm of your voice and be ready for recognizing words.*

At 18 months naming things is a great pleasure and your baby may begin to ask 'What's that?' about everything he sees. He might have a spurt and learn several words in a short time, or he may continue to progress more slowly and steadily. You may hear his first two-word sentences, such as 'Mummy book' – and you need to work out whether he means 'It's Mummy's book,' or 'Give Mummy the book,' or 'Mummy, please read the book.' He may make up his own words for things and be pleased when you follow what he means. He may make a word do general duty, for instance saying 'cat' to mean any animal.

HOW YOU HELP

Your baby needs to listen to language in order to begin to learn, and you provide the major source of raw material for her interested ears. She can't pick out individual words when conversations go on around her, but she will concentrate intently when you speak to her one-to-one, and make eye contact with her.

‘ *Sometimes I have to pay a lot of attention to what I think my baby means because it doesn't come out very clearly, although it really is a word.*

I've noticed with some friends who don't want to use "babytalk" that they speak to their baby just as they would to an adult, using long words and sentences, and they don't pay any attention when their baby makes a sound because it isn't a "real" word yet. Their baby isn't talking yet, and I wonder if it's because he's not getting enough encouragement to have a go. ’ ANNE

Talk to your baby

Don't feel silly talking to your baby while you change her, bathe her, or carry her about the house, even though she can't understand a word of what you are saying. She will show her pleasure as she hears your voice, letting you know she appreciates you chatting with her.

By talking to your baby as you go about everyday routines, describing and naming what you are doing, she will gradually realize that certain sounds always go with certain activities. Soon she will be able to recognize words such as 'bath', 'cup', and 'bed'. By building up her store of familiar words in this way, when she does start to speak for herself she will have a large store of words to put to use.

This doesn't mean that you have to chat away all the time to your baby, which could become forced and awkward for you. There are times where both you and your baby will enjoy a companionable silence. But do think of your baby as an intelligent listener who will enjoy and respond to your comments on your life together.

Baby talk?

Your baby needs to hear language spoken correctly in order to learn herself and you won't be doing her any favours if you use silly names for things. But most parents have an instinctive way of speaking differently to their baby than they would to an adult, which does help a baby to learn.

A baby listens most easily to a slightly high pitched voice, so you might find yourself automatically speaking in a higher voice to your baby. You will

Singing to your baby helps him listen to sounds accurately. The strong rhythm and rhymes catch his attention and when he is only a few months old he may have favourites. He might listen intently, join in with the sounds or jiggle in time.

' *Sarah has just started putting two words together and I'm really enjoying some of the things she comes up with. Often when we're out walking she gets tired or is just too slow to suit me so I ask, "Shall I carry you?" She thinks "carry-you" is a word, so now when she wants to be picked up she holds up her arms and says, "Carry-you me".* ' CAROL

probably exaggerate your facial expressions and the inflections of your voice to make what you are saying seem exciting. You will probably use short, simple sentences and speak fairly slowly and distinctly. Repeating words, especially names of things as your baby looks at them or touches them, will also help her.

As your baby's understanding grows, you are likely to stay one step ahead of her – slowly using longer sentences, adding more descriptive words and speaking in a lower voice. This stretches her listening skills and leads her one step at a time to be able to understand ordinary conversation.

Be responsive

Have you ever tried talking to someone who isn't paying any attention? Chances are you became frustrated and soon gave up. The same is true for your baby, who has no incentive to learn to speak if nobody is listening, but will be encouraged to communicate with you when you show an interest.

In the early stages, being responsive to your baby includes listening to her and showing that you are interested. When you take turns in a cooing or babbling 'conversation', she has the great satisfaction of feeling she has an important part to play. Her gurgling noises are often triggered by having your attention and you looking at her. Listen to her, then copy the sound and wait for her reply. She will recognize her own sound coming from you and will probably do it again.

ENCOURAGING TALKING

◆ *Read books with simple pictures to your baby, repeating the names of objects. You could emphasize something about the object: 'This is a ball. Throw the ball!', or 'It's a red ball'.*

◆ *Take your baby on a walk around the house, finding anything of interest to your baby. Talk about what your baby is looking at.*

◆ *Ask your baby simple questions, even before she can talk. She may be able to point or nod to answer and then you can put it into words for her.*

◆ *Praise your baby's efforts and let her know you think she is clever.*

◆ *Try hard to understand when your baby tries to tell you something.*

◆ *Encourage your baby to speak to other people, but interpret for him since they probably won't understand as well as you do.*

◆ *If someone else looks after your baby, explain what his words or signals are so he can be understood.*

Imitation is a great teacher, and you are the model for your baby's developing language. She will copy not only your words, but also your accent and way of talking. She'll appreciate it if you copy her sometimes, as well.

Later, when your baby first starts to speak her words may be hardly recognizable. She will tend to shorten a word and leave off consonants, so that for 'cat' she says 'ca'. She may also use the wrong name for things, or make up her own words. At this stage if you don't respond to her efforts to communicate, even though they aren't perfect, she will be discouraged from trying. Instead be enthusiastic about her words, and respond in a way that shows you understand her. She will master the finer points later, but for now the important thing is she knows she has communicated with sounds, that you are prepared to make an effort to understand her when it's not immediately clear and that you are pleased with her. If you want to correct her mistakes and help her learn the proper way to pronounce words, it's worth being very tactful about it. She will feel put down and discouraged if you make a point of it, but if you just repeat her words in a friendly way including the correction, she will notice and eventually correct herself.

Expanding baby's skills

Learning is most successful when it starts with what the learner already knows and moves forward one step at a time. Begin with what your baby is already doing, and add one more stage. If your baby is babbling 'ta, ta, ta' you couldn't teach her to say 'rabbit'. But you could imitate her 'ta' and then change it to 'ha, ha', and then 'sa, sa', and she is likely to follow you.

You can also expand on your baby's language when she begins to speak, by repeating what she says in an expanded version. If she says 'Dada', you can reply, 'Yes, there is Daddy's car.' When she says 'Book', you might say, 'Shall we read the book?', or 'It's a nice red book'. By hearing her own statement in an expanded version, she begins to see how to put words together to make her meaning more clear.

Have fun with language

If your baby enjoys language, she will want to share the pleasure with you. Play taking-turn games with sounds and laugh and praise what your baby does. Read nursery rhymes with a rhythm and rhyming pattern that babies enjoy. By about six months your baby will appreciate songs with actions and funny, surprise endings. Your baby will love to hear you sing and even before she can talk she may join in with some of the sounds in a familiar song.

Language for life

Using language enters almost everything we do. The start you provide for your baby in being alert to language so he can learn to use it effectively and with confidence can have a lifelong impact.

We know, for instance, that children who find it easiest to learn to read, and then to do well at school, are those who come to school already enjoying words, with a good ear for sounds and able to express themselves. Children who know nursery rhymes usually learn to read easily, perhaps because they recognize words which sound alike and notice how they are different. All this starts right back in the first year of life, with your first babbled conversations with your baby. On average girls learn to read faster than boys and continue to do better in school, especially in subjects based on language. Could this be linked to the fact that people tend to make more eye contact with girl babies and talk to them more, while with boy babies they are more likely to provide active toys instead of conversation?

Babies differ, and some will grow into people who are good with their hands, some will be athletes, and some will be especially good at communicating with others. Whatever direction your baby eventually chooses, it will be enriched by a good grounding in learning to communicate with you.

Puppets make a good stimulus to a conversation with your baby. Try talking in a different voice as you move the puppet's mouth, and even though he sees your hand go into the puppet he will think it's the puppet who is talking to him.

QUESTIONS AND ANSWERS

Q: My native language is not English and I would like my baby to learn to speak both languages. Will this just confuse him?

A: Babies can be bilingual and your son will learn both languages much more quickly and naturally than if he learned one later in life. It is easier for the baby to sort out the different languages if they are presented to him by separate people. So you could speak to him only in his native language, while his father could speak only English to him. He may be a little slower beginning to talk than if he had only one language to learn, and may mix them up just slightly in the beginning, but very soon he will sort them out and can be at ease in both.

Q: My first child said her first words at eleven months, but my second baby is now 15 months old and hasn't started talking. Is something wrong?

A: It's not unusual for a baby not to start talking until well into the second year. It would be a good idea to ask your GP to check your baby out in case an ear infection has left fluid in the middle ear and is affecting her hearing. Most likely there are other reasons. First children are more likely to talk early and well, probably because they get more one-to-one adult attention. Later children have much more going on around them which can distract them from language, and older children sometimes interpret everything for them so there is no need to speak for themselves. Try to be sure your baby gets your complete attention at a calm time every day.

Q: My baby says several words, but none of them are very clear. Should we correct her and try to get her to say them properly?

A: If you correct your baby when she speaks it might make her think that talking is hard work and you aren't happy with her. It's not worth the risk of spoiling her pleasure in words to insist on proper pronunciation. You can gently guide her by including the words in your reply and she will hear the difference and gradually become more accurate herself. You can also play sound games with her to help her hear and say sounds more accurately – see if she will copy nonsense words like 'fee, tee, hee, bee', or more difficult final consonants like 'mop, mot, mom, mos'.

Q: How soon can you tell if a baby is not hearing properly?

A: It is not always apparent if a baby has hearing problems, because he may hear some types of sound but not others and may respond when you speak to him because he watches your lips move without actually hearing the sounds clearly. A deaf baby will begin to make sounds like any other baby, but by five or six months the babbling won't change to begin to sound like speech, and the sounds will be monotonous. He will also babble less because he can't enjoy hearing the sounds he makes. If you are concerned that your baby may not be reacting to sound, see your doctor who can arrange for special hearing tests. Babies can be fitted with hearing aids when only a few months old and the sooner hearing loss is detected the sooner the baby can learn to talk.

12

Play

‘ *At first he seemed to like his bath just to feel the warm water surrounding him, but now he's discovered that if he flails his arms the water makes a noise and goes flying. He gets so excited and laughs aloud. I have to be prepared to get soaking wet, but we both enjoy it.* ’

WHY PLAY?

A kitten will leap upon a string snaking across the floor, while puppies roll and tumble in a heap of playful yaps, colts kick up their heels and dash across the field – and your baby laughs and gurgles with pleasure as her flailing arms set the toys dancing on her cot mobile. This is play, a crucial ingredient of being young, and it brings delight and satisfaction along with a far more serious purpose.

Play is fun and your baby is drawn to play because she enjoys it. We adults, who separate our time into serious work which must be done and play when our work is finished, may think of play as 'just for fun' – an optional extra. But for your baby playing is far more important than that.

Your baby's job is gradually to become an effective and competent person. She needs to learn about her environment, about how things work, how she can interact with things around her, how to make her body do what she wants it to do, and about living with, and making satisfying relationships with, other people. In all these areas, play is her key.

Through play a baby observes how objects behave. She learns to control her body enough to move objects or make them do something. She can then study them in even more detail. She is drawn by an irresistible drive to explore and manipulate toys and household objects and she has fun doing it. She enjoys it because it satisfies her need to learn and feel effective. So play has built-in enjoyment, but with a serious purpose. Playing is your baby's job.

Directed play?

Because babies learn through play, many toy manufacturers design their products to be educational and parents may come to feel daunted by the responsibility of providing the right toys for their baby to steam ahead in their learning. But most parents have experienced buying an expensive and well-designed toy, only to find that their baby is intrigued with the box or wrapper it came in, while the toy lies ignored on one side.

It is helpful to know which types of activities babies need, so you can provide play opportunities for your baby. But there is no need to direct play in certain directions, or to try to make your baby play with the most clever educational toy instead of an old set of measuring spoons. She has an appetite to learn, and will take advantage of opportunities around her. She knows, more accurately than anyone else can, exactly what kind of play she needs right now in order to develop her skills – and she knows by the pleasure and satisfaction it gives her.

‘ *At three months Thea is too young for a rattle – she doesn't seem to get the idea yet. She's just lying around taking everything in, especially noticing anything that moves. She spends a lot of time watching her own hands, opening and closing them, and I think that is her playing. She also loves it when she hits her mobile and it makes a noise, and she gurgles back at it.* ’ FIONA

160

You don't always need toys for your baby to play with when you are available. Some of her favourite games are likely to be the old standbys – such as peek-a-boo and pat-a-cake. She doesn't find it boring to repeat them, and you will never have such an appreciative audience.

Babies will not make exactly the same choices in play, since they have different personalities, different body types and priorities. Some babies are physically robust and want vigorous physical play; they enjoy being bounced and tossed in the air and are quick to grab, push and throw. Others take quite a while to warm up to physical games, but may love concentrating on a posting box or the sociable pleasure of pat-a-cake. Whatever your baby's preferences, you can help most by providing all types of opportunity for play and then letting her choose which experiences give her most satisfaction now.

YOU ARE THE BEST TOY

A toy is something to play with and a good toy is one that can be used in a variety of ways and inspires new ideas of play. By that definition, you are the best toy of all. Right from the beginning, nothing interests your baby as much as your face and your voice and as she grows there is an infinite variety in how she can play with you.

At first, as with any toy, she observes your characteristics. So she notices the feel of your skin, the rhythm of your heartbeat as you hold her close, your scent. Before long she learns she can have an effect on you – when she cries, you will come, and when she smiles you smile back.

Through playing with you, your baby learns how to interact with other people. She enjoys copy-cat games, peek-a-boo and pat-a-cake. Because she is learning to be sociable, there are times when an activity interests her not so much for its own sake, but because you are sharing it with her.

FUN WITH EVERYDAY OBJECTS

Your baby is interested in anything and everything and will play with all sorts of things you have around the house. Kitchen things are especially varied and interesting. For instance:

- *yogurt pots*
- *spoons – wooden and metal*
- *set of plastic measuring spoons*
- *egg carton*
- *colander*
- *key-ring*
- *cardboard box*
- *small plastic bottles*
- *cotton reels, single or several tied on a string*
- *coloured plastic plates or bowls*

- *ice-cube tray*
- *spatula*
- *pots and pans with lids*
- *plastic biscuit cutters*
- *cassette tape boxes*
- *cellotape roll*
- *funnel*
- *pieces of fabric*
- *toilet roll tube*
- *empty margarine containers*
- *washing up mop*

You also bring experiences to her. When she is a few weeks old, you move a rattle across her vision for her eyes to track, perhaps shaking it gently so she associates what she sees with the direction sounds come from. Later you show her interesting things she has never seen before and join in with her until she is able to play with them on her own. You watch for the signs of boredom and show her a new aspect to revive her interest in a familiar toy, or offer her some new ideas of what she can explore.

Your baby doesn't need you to play with her and entertain her all the time, though. There are other things you need to do, and you want some time to yourself. Your baby can be involved in playing by herself, but she still enjoys your companionship and will be happiest if she can see and hear you nearby. You might enjoy getting together with another parent and baby, or a mother-baby group, where you can be near and interact with your baby now and then, and at the same time enjoy some adult conversation.

PLAYING AND GROWING

Birth to three months: Your baby is interested in watching anything which moves, so let him watch you and other family members as they go about their activities. Place him where he can see the laundry flapping on the line or tree branches swaying.

He doesn't really need toys at this stage, but he might like a very light-weight rattle which he will grasp and may be able to put to his mouth – but he may also hit himself on the head with it. He will also appreciate brightly coloured patterns on a cot bumper, or soft toys or pictures in books which you can prop up for him to look at.

You can make a cot mobile by tying some elastic across the cot and securely hanging objects from it. You could tie on a rattle, large bright beads, a bunch of keys, a cotton reel, a fluffy ball, shiny foil tart tins or brightly coloured cards. Three or four objects are enough at a time and you can substitute something new for one of the objects every few days, or tie something new on to one of the items.

• TOYS: *Rattle, mobiles, music box, soft toy.*

Four to six months: Now your baby can reach and grasp objects, and will enjoy feeling different shapes and textures, and making things happen. Toys which squeak, ring or rattle when moved will give satisfaction. He is interested in faces and expressions and will enjoy playing with his reflection in a mirror when you hold him up to look. He can now grasp objects suspended within reach above him and will put them in his mouth, so doublecheck that anything you fasten on his cot mobile is safe. When he discovers his feet, at about five months, you can hang toys within reach of his feet for him to kick.

• TOYS: *Rattles, teething rings, squeezy-squeaky toys, soft irregularly shaped balls, soft doll, bright wooden beads on a string.*

Play gives a chance to try out new experiences, and imagination is often the biggest ingredient. A baby 'brumming' a car on the floor can imagine it is real and has the powerful feeling of 'driving'. With a little imagination, a big cardboard box is something special – a den-like place with doors.

Six to ten months: Your baby is learning to control his hands and fingers and enjoys exploring objects of all types and making a noise with them. Once he can sit up, the range of things he can play with increases. He will enjoy pop-up toys which bounce when he pushes them or a music box with a string he can pull. You can give him a box containing squares of cloth of different colours and textures. A baby bouncer or baby walker may be enjoyed for short periods at a time.

• TOYS: *Activity centre, balls, unbreakable baby mirror, nesting toys, large ball.*

Ten to 12 months: Hand movements are more coordinated, and your baby will enjoy turning, stacking, investigating shapes of objects and putting things inside containers. He will also enjoy being involved in household jobs and will 'help' you put shopping away, put the washing in the machine, put groceries in your trolley, or vegetables in the pot. Now that he's mobile, he will enjoy toys he can push or pull and toys on a string he can drag along the floor to him. He can now hold chalks, crayons or pens, but will have most luck making a mark with felt-tips – be sure they contain washable ink and don't leave him alone with them. Water play develops now that he can sit in the bath.

• TOYS: *Small bricks, posting box, stacking toys, trolley, kitchen utensils, toy xylophone, water toys and beakers for the bath, bag or small basket to put things in.*

Twelve to 18 months: Your baby is becoming much more competent at using his body and will want to practise with activities that develop his muscles, judgement of distances and balance. He may discover an activity like stepping on and off a low box, or walking with your slippers on. A small push-along bike will give him practice at physical skills. As well as boisterous play for his large muscles, he enjoys quieter play which develops his fine muscle control.

Babies take an interest in other babies, and usually enjoy the companionship of playing alongside each other. They may watch each other's activities and copy what they see another baby doing, though it will probably be some time before they learn to cooperate enough to actually play together.

SAFETY TIPS

◆ *When you buy toys or play equipment, check for a safety label.*
◆ *With secondhand toys, check there are no loose parts or broken edges.*
◆ *Never give your baby something with hard sharp edges.*
◆ *Don't give your baby anything small or with small parts which could come off and be swallowed.*
◆ *With soft toys, check for safety of eyes and noses. They should be embroidered on, or fixed with safety backings so they won't come off.*
◆ *Be careful with items which could come apart when chewed, such as the cardboard of toilet paper rolls or magazine pages, and take them away once they are softened.*
◆ *Don't leave your baby alone when playing, except in a cot or playpen with the safest of toys such as a rattle or board book.*

He wants you nearby for companionship and needs you to supervise for safety, but he may play for extended periods on his own. He experiments in his play, as he wants to understand how things work. He is becoming able to pretend and may enjoy toy cars, animals, teddy and dolls. He can begin to play with sand – you can buy silver sand and put it in a washing-up basin on a spread of newspapers – but watch closely and teach him not to put it in his mouth. Thick paintbrushes and bold poster paint on large paper give him pleasure in watching the record it makes of his arm and hand movements.

• *TOYS: Hammer toys, toy telephone, doll, animals, cars, bike, mouth organ, paints, simple inset jigsaw with chunky pieces, books, water toys with holes.*

ENJOYING BOOKS

As soon as you can hold your baby on your lap and show her a book, you can introduce her to the pleasure of books and reading. When she is very young, perhaps two or three months old, she will enjoy looking at books because of the colours and patterns on the pages, the sound of the turning pages and the comfort of being held closely and hearing your voice. At that stage you can show her any books or magazines which have pictures.

By about six months, you might read together from a book of nursery rhymes, and she will enjoy the rhythmic sounds and the pictures, though she still won't recognize anything more than colours and pattern.

Towards the end of the first year your baby can begin to recognize simple pictures in books. Colourful photos or lifelike drawings of familiar everyday objects are easiest for your baby to recognize instead of cartoon-type drawings. Talk about the pictures with her, and point as you name things. Ask her questions and she may begin to point in reply, or make sound effects.

Books offer the chance to be involved with things beyond your everyday life, and your baby may come to recognize and enjoy making sounds for farm or jungle animals, a steam train, a fire engine. Everyday subjects like mealtimes or a baby going to bed will also be appreciated.

She will enjoy hearing you read real stories earlier than you may expect, and though she may not understand much of it, her understanding will gradually grow. From about 12 months onwards, your baby may enjoy stories with familiar elements like parents and babies, bathtime, bedtime, shopping and playing – whether the characters are people or animals. She loves repetition and though you may tire of saying exactly the same words and singing exactly the same nursery rhymes day after day, she won't be bored.

Learning to love books is the beginning of a lifetime's reward and respecting books can be part of the earliest lessons. A tattered, scribbled-on book with dog-eared cover or no cover at all, thrown at random in a box of toys, does not command respect. But books which are kept in good order and belong in a certain place will become valued objects and the pleasures they have to offer are then open to your baby.

Babies love to crinkle paper, and if left alone with a book they will soon screw up the pages and probably tear some. As well as giving the wrong message about respect for books, you will not be likely to buy many books if that is their fate.

' *Gregory loved books as soon as he could sit up. It teaches him words, as we point to things. I love those lovely books with a photograph of a cat or a plant. Because he sees us read, he sits around reading in his way, and it's nice when you see him doing something you like to do. He has his own bookshelf in the kitchen where we spend a lot of time, and sometimes I take some away or put new ones out.* ' SUE

Instead, young babies can be given cloth books, which provide bright pictures and a chance to turn pages. By about nine or ten months, books with board pages can be handled by a baby alone. Books with paper pages can be reserved for reading with you until your baby is over one year old.

OUT AND ABOUT

Once your baby becomes mobile, either crawling or beginning to walk, being confined in a pram or pushchair for long periods is very frustrating. It helps if you plan outings for off-peak times to avoid crowds, noise and confusion. Then you are able to take your time and involve your baby in what you are doing, whether it is talking about the items on the supermarket shelf or dawdling to look at the water running down the edge of the street or the blossoms opening on a bush on the way home.

For car journeys your baby must of course remain in an approved infant seat. Again, a young baby is likely to be lulled to sleep by the movement and continuous sound of the car. As your baby gets older you will probably find it useful to keep a few toys in the car to produce as necessary, and you could plan long journeys to include frequent breaks and perhaps night-time travel so he is more likely to sleep.

Warm weather gives the chance to play outside. Even a young baby will enjoy the sights and sounds when lying or sitting on a blanket in the garden. Once he is mobile there is plenty to investigate outside, but you will have to keep a careful watch to ensure he doesn't pick up small pebbles or anything else to put in his mouth. Don't let him play on lawns which dogs might have fouled as dog faeces presents a health risk and children are especially vulnerable.

Energetic toddlers love the freedom and adventure of playing outdoors. Gardens, however, hold many hidden dangers for young explorers, so make sure your child is always carefully supervised and never leave her alone near water.

PLAYFUL EXERCISE

Physical movement is fun and is one form of play for your baby. By doing exercises with your baby, you can help her physical development. But just as you probably enjoy exercise more in the context of a game rather than just as a way to stay fit, remember that the main purpose with your baby should be for her to enjoy it.

Birth to three months: The simplest form of exercise, which your baby should ideally have everyday, is a period of free movement on a flat surface, without too much restriction from clothes. A very young baby may not like the feeling of exposure when undressed, but as soon as she is comfortable without a nappy you can put her on the floor on a waterproof pad or folded towel, wearing perhaps only a vest, and let her kick and move freely for a quarter of an hour or so. Babies often enjoy a vigorous kicking session when they are dry and fresh after a bath.

Some of your postnatal exercises can include your baby. Try holding your baby on your tummy as you do curl-ups, or on your lap with bottom walking. As your baby adjusts to your movement, she will be strengthening her own muscles.

- Arm raises – with your baby lying on her back, let her grasp your fingers in each hand. Raise her arms over her head, then lower again.
- Knee bends – holding your baby's lower legs, bend her knees and bring them up toward her chest. Then bring them back down, straightening her legs.
- Sit-ups – you can help your baby's head control with early sit-ups. With your baby lying on her back along your lap, hold her hands and slowly raise her. At first you will have to use one hand to support her head and neck as you lower her carefully, but as her strength increases you can just lower her slowly.
- Head raising – to help build strength in your baby's back, roll a shawl or towel to a thickness of about 6 cm (2½ in) and place it on the floor. Lower your baby on to her front with the towel under her shoulders and her arms forward on the floor. Then talk to her to get her attention so she lifts her head. Another approach is to lie comfortably on your back on a sofa, place your baby on her front on top of you and talk to her so she takes her weight on her forearms and raises her head to look at you.
- Hip swings – when your baby has developed some head control, hold her upright with your hands around her chest and gently tilt her side to side in a swinging motion, so her legs swing freely. Be careful to keep her head in line with her back, not tilting too far so her head drops sideways.

Older babies: Your baby will continue to enjoy some time on the floor with a minimum of clothes and to be involved in your own exercises.

- Aeroplane – you could try lying on your back with your knees to your chest and lay your baby on her front along your shins. Hold her under her arms as you raise and lower your lower legs, tipping her back and forth or bouncing her gently. You will be strengthening your own abdominal muscles and thighs, while your baby strengthens her back and neck.

Babies have tremendous flexibility which regular use of the full range of movement will help to maintain. As your baby becomes more physically active, her muscles strengthen, while stretching will keep them supple.

- Bicycle – with your baby on her back, hold one of her lower legs in each hand and move her legs gently in a cycling movement, first as if cycling forward, and then as if cycling backward.
- Toes to nose – clasp your baby's calves with each hand and gently bring one foot up toward her nose while the other leg lifts off the floor. Then lower the first leg and repeat with the other.
- Seesaw – a variation of sit-ups and even more fun if you sing 'seesaw, Marjorie Daw'. Lie on your back with feet on the floor and your knees bent. Sit your baby on your stomach and hold her hands. Begin to seesaw by curling your head and shoulders off the floor, leaning your baby back on your knees as you come up and pulling her forward as you go down.
- Wheelbarrow – once your baby has good arm strength and can take some of her weight on her arms, place her on her front and lift her bottom and legs as you hold her lower body. She may be able to take a step or two with her hands.

BABY MASSAGE

Another enjoyable activity to do with your baby is massage. If you massage your baby regularly he will enjoy it as a quiet, relaxing time. A backrub can become a means of calming and settling him right through childhood. It is best for your baby to be naked so after a bath or while changing clothes is a good time. A warm, quiet room, perhaps with relaxing music and subdued light, will set the right atmosphere.

You can learn specific techniques for massaging babies, but equally you can discover for yourself what your baby likes. Basically you are just stroking your baby and can do what comes naturally. Relax with a breath out, and hold your baby across your lap or on the floor. Massage with bare hands or use a little vegetable oil so the strokes glide smoothly. Be sure your hands are warm and if you use oil warm it on your hands first. Use light, steady pressure at first and increase it as you gain confidence about what your baby enjoys. Each movement should be slow and repeated several times.

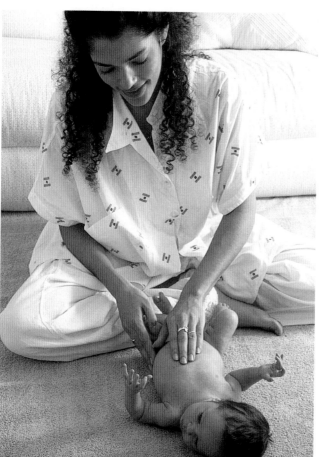

Massage techniques

Abdomen: *Massage in large circles with both hands, stroking down the centre of your baby's belly and up around the sides.*

Back: *Stroke with both hands down the centre of his back and then up the sides. Circle with your thumbs between his shoulder blades and use your palm to rub in a circle around the small of his back.*

Legs: *Stroke down the back of his legs and then lightly stroke from the top of his back down his legs. On first the lower leg and then the thigh, circle up the inside and then back down along the outside.*

Arms: *Stroke down the outer arm, and then very gently up the inner arm to his elbow.*

QUESTIONS AND ANSWERS

Q: How old should my baby be before I can take her swimming?

A: Once she has had her first set of immunizations you can take your baby to a public swimming bath. The water and surrounding air temperatures should both be warm, but even so your baby may get cold fairly quickly so the swimming session should be short. Introduce her to the water by holding her with the water around you, and when she is relaxed you can let her float on her back in the water as you support her. Babies who are introduced to swimming early usually feel at home in water and don't have to overcome fear later.

Q: At eight months my baby hardly sleeps during the day and I spend all my time trying to entertain him. How can I run a household and make sure he doesn't get bored?

A: One possibility is to include him in household jobs. Sit him near you, give him something to play with and talk to him while you work. When you have a job to do, you can plan ahead to create some time when he'll be occupied. Settle him nearby with something you know he enjoys, and perhaps put on a tape of music or nursery rhymes. He might like to sit in a big cardboard box with a toy. While you get on with your work, show interest in what he is doing and talk to him occasionally. Keep an eye out and change his activity just before he gets restless.

Q: Our sitting room looks like a bomb site when Jane, 15 months, has been playing. Should we try to keep it tidy or let it go?

A: Too much clutter gets in the way of good play and you'll find Jane concentrates more when the room is tidier. It also gets to be a safety hazard when the floor is full of toys. Jane can learn now that things have a place in which they belong and you can begin to let her know she is responsible for putting them there. You could keep a toy box in the sitting room, and now and then offer to help her put toys away – she will enjoy doing it with you.

Q: I would like to use my imagination and save money on toys by making them myself, but since they haven't been checked for safety like commercial ones will it be OK to give them to my baby?

A: You do need to be careful about homemade toys, but they are sometimes the best of all. Just as with any household items you let your baby play with, you will have to use common sense about whether any small parts or bits of fluff could come off, or whether there are any sharp edges or corners, and keep an eye out in case items deteriorate and become unsafe.

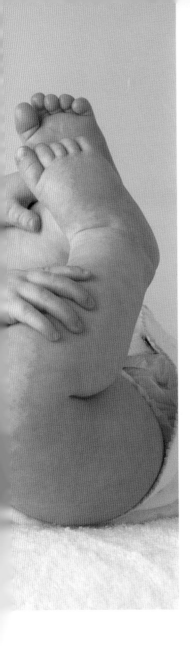

13

Health Care

' *One night Josie woke up screaming and she felt very hot and kept holding her hands on top of her head. I tried to settle her, but she just kept crying. Finally I rang the doctor, who came out to see us in the middle of the night. He reassured me that I'd been right to ring. He said her tonsils were infected, which can cause a bad headache, and gave us some antibiotics to start right away. It's so hard to know what's wrong when they're too little to tell you.* '

YOUR ROLE AS A PARENT

Health care professionals are expert helpers in guarding your baby's physical well-being, but as in every other area of your baby's life, your care is the cornerstone. Whether feeding, changing a nappy, settling him to sleep, or fitting a stair gate, you are looking after his health.

Being healthy does not mean just being free from illness. In fact, a healthy baby – just as a healthy adult – is likely occasionally to have a tummy bug or catch a cold. But a healthy baby will not fall prey to every possible disease-carrying germ which comes his way and will be able to throw off an illness and bounce back fairly quickly. You are helping your baby build up a healthy resistance to disease when you make sure he has a good diet, enough rest, exercise to stimulate all his body functions, and isn't put under strain by an environment that is too hot or too cold.

You also protect your baby as far as possible from the sources of ill health. By keeping his surroundings clean and taking care with hygiene especially with bottlefeeding or preparing baby food, you limit his exposure to germs. And you protect him from accidents – anticipating dangers so you can child-proof your house, and keeping an eye on safety in all his play.

When a minor health problem arises, such as nappy rash, you probably deal with it yourself. You also notice when something is more seriously amiss and make the decision of when to call the doctor. At times of illness you take on the role of nurse, looking after your baby with your doctor's help and advice.

PROFESSIONAL HEALTH CARE

For the first few days of your baby's life a midwife, trained in the care of newborns, will keep an eye on your baby's well-being and be available for answering your health questions. She will visit you at home during the first ten days of your baby's life. The midwife then hands over responsibility as your first port of call to the health visitor. The health visitor is trained in baby and child care and family health. She will see you and your baby in your home and she may also be available at a baby clinic and by telephone when-ever you want information or advice.

Your family doctor is also available by telephone if your baby seems unwell and may give you advice or ask you to bring him to the surgery. If your baby is too ill to go to the doctor or needs to be seen out of surgery hours the doctor may make a house call. The GP may be involved in giving your baby his immunizations and regular developmental checks and can arrange for a specialist medical opinion and help if required.

Baby clinic

Baby clinics are organized to help keep babies healthy, and may be held in your doctor's surgery or in a local Health Authority building – your health visitor should be able to tell you where your nearest clinic is held.

The well-baby clinic gives you the chance to seek advice from health visitors and doctors. While your baby is young he will be weighed at each visit. The clinic may offer developmental checks, to keep track of your baby reaching milestones at roughly the right times or they may be performed by your health visitor at home or by your own doctor. Immunizations may also be done at the clinic or through your doctor.

' We used to worry a lot about germs and sterilize everything he came in contact with. But after a while we became more relaxed, and if he dropped something we'd just give it a quick wash off and hand it back. He's got to get used to ordinary household germs, and once they're getting around you can't worry about everything being one hundred per cent hygienic. ' SHEILA

Many parents appreciate the baby clinic as a meeting place with other parents and babies, and some clinics run organized mother-baby groups. The chance to talk over your situation with others and make new friends can be a worthwhile aspect of the baby clinic, especially if you have recently given up work and are feeling isolated at home.

With a young baby, and at times when you have any particular worries, you might want to make a weekly visit to the baby clinic. Later on, or if you already have children and feel fairly confident on your own, you might prefer to go just at specific times for immunizations or developmental checks – your health visitor will advise you about when these are due. The clinic is there for you to use in the way that suits you best.

At a well-baby clinic your health visitor can show you where your baby's weight and height fall on the range of normal growth patterns. Your baby's gains are unlikely to be completely steady, and it doesn't matter if he is large or small compared to other babies, as long as his average progress shows regular growth.

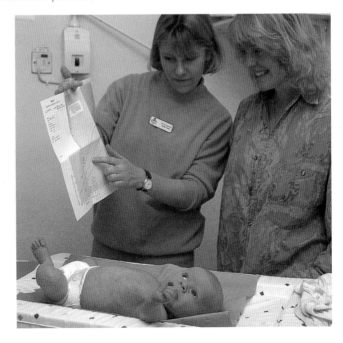

IMMUNIZATIONS

For some infectious diseases, immunizations protect your baby from becoming seriously ill. Your baby receives a vaccine containing a tiny dose of an organism, which stimulates his immune system to produce antibodies against it. These stay in his bloodstream as a defence against the organism in the future.

Immunizations are given by injection or by mouth and contain either a live but inactive organism, or an organism which has been killed. The organism is one which would cause the disease or a closely related one. Some immunizations need only one dose, while others such as polio must be given in a series.

The schedule of immunizations may vary somewhat from one area to another, but the usual pattern is to give one combined injection containing vaccines for diphtheria, tetanus and pertussis (whooping cough) and Hib (haemophilus influenzae b, a bacterial infection that can cause a range of illnesses including meningitis and pneumonia) together with meningitis C at two months, three months and four months. A polio vaccine will also be given as drops in the mouth on each of these occasions. At about 12–15 months, a combined measles, mumps and rubella (German measles) vaccination (MMR) is given. This completes the immunization pattern for your baby, until boosters are needed at age four or five years. Your doctor or clinic will probably give you a booklet to record your baby's immunizations, which you can keep up to date and refer to in the future.

When not to immunize

If your baby has diarrhoea, vomiting or a fever, or is showing the first signs of a cough or runny nose, your doctor will probably delay giving a vaccine until he has recovered. A runny nose or cough which is clearly a cold and not initial signs of another illness, is usually not a reason to delay an immunization. Tell your doctor about any symptoms your baby may have, and she will advise you as to whether it affects the timing of immunizations.

Some babies should not receive immunizations because of possibly greater risks of serious reactions. If a baby has had a severe reaction to a vaccination before, he should not have it repeated. Tell your doctor if your baby suffered any damage to the nervous system at birth, shows any signs of not developing properly, has had fits or has any known allergies. In these situations your doctor might want to seek specialist advice before advising you further about whether to give the immunization, particularly the whooping cough portion of the vaccine.

' I was very concerned about giving Jessica the immunizations and took a lot of convincing, probably because I had worked with vaccine-damaged children. My wife was quite clear that we should go ahead, but I was convinced after I had a chat with our GP and he explained about the social responsibility of avoiding epidemics. It seemed selfish then not to go ahead. She was off colour for about three weeks after the MMR, but didn't have any reaction with the others. ' ANDREW

Simple drops by mouth of the polio vaccine protect children against polio, a disease which crippled children in epidemics before the immunization was developed. Even though polio is now rare, immunizations must be kept up to prevent it once again sweeping through a community.

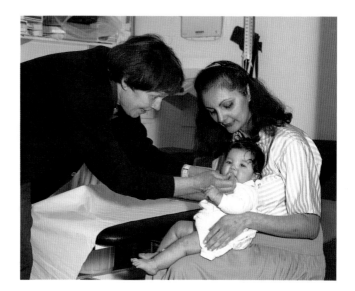

Reactions

Parents sometimes worry about giving their baby immunizations through fear of reactions. It is true that no vaccine can be guaranteed to be one hundred per cent without harmful effects, but it is a matter of weighing the risks against the benefits. Most of the vaccines are extremely safe and all are judged to provide protection that outweighs the risk of permanent harm. The diseases prevented by immunization are not mild childhood illnesses, but can cause death and permanent disability. The risks from the diseases are far greater than the very slight risks from the vaccines and unless most children are immunized against a disease it can sweep through a community, causing a tremendous amount of suffering. Rarely, a child can still get a disease after being vaccinated against it, but it is almost always a milder case.

After a vaccination, you may notice no reaction at all in your baby. It is quite common, though, for a baby to be restless and feverish a few hours later. Less commonly, a baby may scream and develop a red swelling around the site of the injection. This is not a reaction that you need be too concerned about and you can just try to make your baby more comfortable, perhaps giving a dose of paracetamol and a cool drink of water, and sponging his arms and legs with tepid water if he is feverish. Contact your doctor if you are worried or if fever and crying last more than 24 hours. Very rarely a baby will have a more serious reaction. If your baby shows any of the following signs after immunization you should contact your GP immediately or take your baby to hospital:

- high-pitched scream
- limpness
- pale or blue skin
- convulsions
- loss of consciousness

Do not repeat the vaccine if your baby has had any of these reactions.

IS MY BABY ILL?

Because you know your baby so well, you will notice small changes that might indicate your baby is ill. Often her behaviour is the first clue – she may be irritable, wake and cry more often than usual or be unusually sleepy, take little interest in things around her, lose her appetite or whimper miserably.

If you suspect your baby may be unwell, do take it seriously. Because a baby's body is small, with little reserve of energy and body fluids, an illness can develop quickly and have serious effects more rapidly than it would in an older person.

Calling the doctor

If you are concerned that your baby seems unwell or she shows any signs of illness don't hesitate to call your doctor thinking it may be too trivial for medical attention. Doctors know that illness can take hold quickly in babies, and would rather be consulted early rather than later when it may have become more serious. Often all that is needed is advice over the telephone, and encouragement to ring back if no improvement is seen.

WHEN TO CONTACT THE DOCTOR

Contact your doctor right away if your baby:
◆ *Is unconscious, or semi-conscious and difficult to rouse.*
◆ *Has a convulsion.*
◆ *Cries in pain and won't be comforted.*
◆ *Is floppy.*
◆ *Has difficulty breathing, with either rapid or forced breaths.*
◆ *Goes blue or very pale.*
◆ *Vomits continuously for more than an hour.*
◆ *Has a very weak cry or piercing high-pitched cry.*
◆ *Has a fontanelle (soft spot on the head) which bulges or is sunken.*
◆ *A dry mouth or sunken eyes.*

Contact your doctor within a day if your baby:
◆ *Shows a marked change in behaviour – is irritable, miserable or lethargic.*
◆ *Has vomiting and/or diarrhoea which is still present after six hours.*
◆ *Has a high temperature, 38-39°C (100-102°F); feels hot and sweaty.*
◆ *Refuses to feed.*
◆ *Develops a rash that you can't account for.*
◆ *Has a cough or cold if under six months.*
◆ *Has a cough together with wheezing, barking or vomiting.*
◆ *Has lumps (swollen glands) in the neck, armpits or groin.*

Illnesses are often most worrying at night, and it can be difficult to know whether to ring for advice during the night or wait until morning. See the chart opposite for guidance about when it can wait, and when you should ring regardless of the time. Your doctor may have a telephone relaying system at night to divert calls to the doctor on duty, so don't hang up but wait for a reply.

'*From the age of nine months Gareth lived off antibiotics, because he had constant ear infections. I could tell right away because he'd get irritable and shake his head, and when I'd take him in to the doctor he'd say "Oh no, not again". It only stopped when he had grommets put in his ears when he was just two. Now I wish I'd looked into whether it could be an allergy reaction that was causing the congestion in his tubes.* ' JANE

Be prepared to describe to your doctor the signs you have noticed in your baby, when it first started, whether she seems to be getting worse and anything you have already done for her.

NURSING YOUR ILL BABY

When your baby is ill she doesn't know why she feels so bad and parents can feel helpless in the face of an illness that is taking its course. But far from being helpless, whatever medical care may be required ·your tender loving care is still the best thing to help your baby through a difficult time. She relies on you for courage, trusting that it will be all right, and for finding what peace she can in the midst of her discomfort.

If your baby has to go into hospital, you can stay with her and give her the security of your presence, having you manage most of her routine care. She should be in a ward specially designed for babies and children, with provision for parents. Most hospitals would encourage a parent to stay overnight, but even if that is not the case you do have a right to do so. Talk to the ward sister and your GP if you are not happy about arrangements in the hospital.

When looking after your baby at home, you can largely take your lead from her. Don't worry if she doesn't want to eat much – she'll make up for it when she's better. She may want to be held much of the time, or may find the physical contact tiring and prefer lying down on her own. She may want to play, but need more attention than usual to help her overcome the grizzliness of feeling off colour.

Sickness and diarrhoea

A bout of sickness or diarrhoea is quite common and usually short-lived so you can care for your baby yourself. Try to keep her on clear fluids (including very dilute fruit juice) or breastmilk only until the vomiting or diarrhoea stop. Then, if bottlefeeding, re-introduce milk diluted to no more than half strength at first. If breastfeeding, be careful about possible irritating foods in your diet, such as highly spiced food, onions and peppers. Consult your doctor

FIRST AID

Artificial respiration
This information should not be considered a substitute for proper training, however you should read through it in case an accident or emergency occurs.

◆ *If your baby stops breathing but has a circulation you will need to breathe air into his lungs (artificial ventilation, pic 1 below). Send someone for medical help if possible.*

◆ *Lie him on his back, tilt his head back and place your mouth over his mouth and nose.*

◆ *Use a shallow breath, just enough to make his chest rise slightly, as you breathe out into his lungs. Remove your mouth to allow his chest to relax as you take a fresh breath.*

◆ *Continue until he breathes on his own or help arrives.*

◆ *If your baby isn't breathing and has no circulation you will need to breathe into his lungs and also give chest compressions (pic 2). Place the tips of two fingers on the lower breastbone and press down sharply. Do this five times in three seconds.*

◆ *Alternate one breath of artificial ventilation with five chest compressions until help arrives.*

1

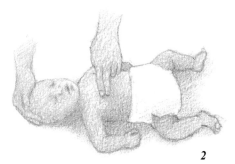

2

Burns
◆ *For serious burns, cover with a sterile dressing and get medical help immediately.*

◆ *For minor burns and scalds, use cold water only – no ointments or creams.*

◆ *With scalds, remove any hot wet clothing unless it is stuck to the skin.*

◆ *Hold burned area under cold running water for up to ten minutes.*

Grazes and cuts
◆ *Clean grazes with water, wiping away from the wound. Leave uncovered to heal.*

◆ *Press a clean cloth onto a cut to stop bleeding.*

◆ *Wash with warm water, dry and apply a plaster.*

◆ *If bleeding does not stop easily or a cut looks serious, seek medical aid.*

Poisoning
◆ *Try to find out what your child has taken and how much.*

◆ *Take the container or substance with you and take your baby to the doctor or casualty department of a hospital.*

◆ *Do not try to make your child sick as this can cause more harm.*

FIRST AID

Choking
◆ See if you can hook the object back out of his mouth with your finger. If it doesn't come immediately, don't keep trying and risk pushing it further in.

◆ Lay the baby along your forearm, facing downwards, supporting his chin (pic 1). Give five sharp slaps on his back.

◆ If this fails to loosen the obstruction, turn him face up on your other arm, supporting his head. Place two fingers low on the breastbone and give five sharp downward thrusts (pic 2). If there is still a blockage, send someone for medical help.

1

2

Electric shock
◆ Switch off the power.

◆ Don't use direct contact to pull your baby away from the electric source, because he may be 'live'. Push him away from it with a non-conductor of electricity such as a broom or seat cushion.

◆ Check that he is breathing. If not, give artificial respiration.

◆ Call your doctor.

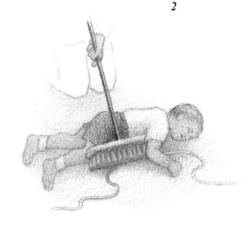

Recovery position
◆ If your child is unconscious but breathing, or very drowsy after an accident, place him in the recovery position while you await medical help.

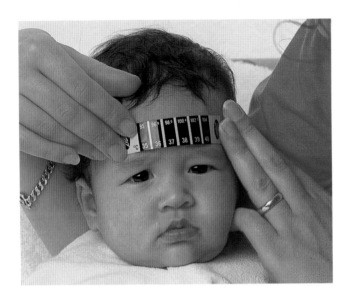

A fever strip is a quick way to discover whether your baby has a temperature or, just as significant, a temperature lower than normal. A baby's temperature can go up or down rapidly, but it is a good piece of information to give your doctor if your baby looks feverish and seems unwell.

if the situation has not resolved after six hours. He may prescribe a drink to prevent dehydration.

See your doctor if your baby shows signs of projectile vomiting, where the milk is forcefully vomited across the room. In a baby between about two and six weeks this may be a sign of pyloric stenosis, an obstruction of the valve outlet of the stomach, which may require surgical repair.

Fever
When your baby is feverish, feeling burning hot to the touch and shivery or shaky, try to cool him by using only lightweight clothing and bedcovers and keeping the room pleasantly warm but not hot. Give extra drinks and you can give a dose of paracetamol syrup. Sponge his arms and legs with lukewarm water, or put him in a lukewarm bath.

When a baby's temperature goes very high he may have a fever fit. Though very frightening to witness, the baby will come out of the fit on his own and recover completely. Stay with him, lie him on his side and be sure nothing is against his nose and mouth to block his breathing. When the fit has finished he will be drowsy or fall deep asleep. Ask someone to call the doctor when the fit starts, or ring yourself afterwards if you are on your own.

Coughs and colds
Give your baby plenty of drinks and provide extra moisture in the air with a water vaporizer or boiling a kettle in his room (stay with it, and be sure it is out of reach if your baby is mobile). Don't use cough medicines unless prescribed by your doctor. See your doctor if a cold starts to get worse after the first few days, since a bacterial infection may have developed.

ACCIDENT PREVENTION

It's a rare baby who never experiences any sort of accident, since the world around us, other people, and babies themselves are not totally predictable. In most cases the accident is a small thing such as an item dropped on a baby or a newly-sitting baby toppling backward to bump her head.

Protecting your baby is one of your most important jobs as a parent, and the risk of serious accident must always be borne in mind. Major accidents to babies do occur with tragic frequency, and although it is impossible to remove all risks, most serious accidents could be avoided with proper care.

Go through your home room by room, checking for possible hazards. These include things which are dangerous for you as well as for a crawling or toddling baby, such as loose rugs or clutter on the floor which could trip you up – if you were carrying your baby you could both go down, or you could drop or spill something onto her.

Think ahead of your baby's development, so you can baby-proof your home ready for what she may be able to do next. She may learn to climb up to an open window or open a screw top before you have realized she could. Waiting until you see what she can do may be too late.

Safety equipment minimizes risk. In the car use approved car seats appropriate to your baby's age and weight. The kitchen is the most dangerous room in the house, so use a playpen in the corner or a safety gate across the door so your baby is not underfoot when you are busy.

Be sure all equipment for your baby is safe. All new equipment should meet safety standards and have a clear mark of approval. Babies usually don't wear out equipment since they grow and change so fast, and handed-down equipment and toys can save money and offer your baby a bigger range. But check carefully to see that any secondhand equipment is in good condition with no loose parts, cracks or worn joints.

Most accidents happen not on average days when life flows smoothly, but at times of stress such as when your baby is ill or tired, something special is going on so people are distracted, or you are upset. At times like these remember to remain alert to your baby's safety.

Within a safe place to play, your baby can explore in some freedom. You can also promote her safety by not just saying 'no' to dangerous things, but telling her why so she begins to be aware of safety for herself.

HOME SAFETY

◆ *Think ahead as to your baby's next stage of development and child-proof your home before there is a risk.*

◆ *Remove breakable objects from your baby's reach, remembering that she will soon be able to climb.*

◆ *Fit safety gates on stairs, top and bottom.*

◆ *Use fireguards around open fires.*

◆ *Keep all dangerous or poisonous substances out of your baby's reach.*

◆ *Fit babyproof catches on cupboards containing anything breakable or dangerous.*

◆ *Keep items small enough to be swallowed out of reach.*

◆ *Use safety plugs in unused electric sockets.*

◆ *Don't let electric wires lie along the floor.*

◆ *Remove furniture with sharp corners, or use safety corners.*

◆ *Never leave hot things in the room with your baby.*

◆ *Use a cooker guard.*

◆ *Turn all pan handles toward the back of the cooker.*

◆ *Put transfers on glass doors so your baby can see them.*

◆ *Don't use overhanging tablecloths which can be pulled down.*

◆ *Keep floors uncluttered and fasten rugs down so they don't slip.*

◆ *Check all equipment for a kitemark of approval and check old toys and equipment for hazards from wear.*

◆ *Strap your baby in a highchair and be sure it is almost impossible to tip in case she tries to climb in.*

◆ *Accidents are more likely when your baby is ill or tired, or there is confusion or upset in the home, so try to keep things calm and keep a careful watch on things.*

QUESTIONS AND ANSWERS

Q: Can alternative medicines be used for babies?

A: Yes, some alternative therapies can be of help with health problems in babies. Homeopathic remedies, for instance, are non-toxic and safe and often show immediate benefits. Contact the British Homeopathic Association (see Appendix) for information about home use, or how to contact a professional homeopath. Some parents have found cranial osteopathy to be of help with crying babies and sleep problems, as well as other conditions. Just because something is 'natural', however, it is not necessarily safe for babies, so beware of herbal mixtures not intended for babies. Your GP is a good first contact when your baby is ill and then you could go on to consider alternative remedies especially for longer term problems.

Q: How should I take my baby's temperature?

A: It is not usually necessary to know the exact temperature, because a baby's temperature can go up and down quite rapidly and not necessarily give an accurate indication about illness. You can tell when your baby is feverish because she will feel very hot to the touch and her eyes may look burning and shiny. As well as fever, a temperature that is lower than normal can be an important sign of illness. A normal temperature is 36°-37.5°C (97-99.5°F).

A fever strip which you hold on your baby's forehead (see page 182) is the easiest way to take her temperature. Otherwise, you can hold a thermometer in her armpit, with her arm pressed against her side to keep in her body heat, for two minutes.

Q: My baby has a cold and keeps breaking off trying to feed because he can't breathe. What should I do?

A: You could try to help your baby breathe more freely by holding him in a warm steamy atmosphere for a few minutes before a feed, for instance in the bathroom with the hot taps or shower running. If he is still too congested to feed easily, see your doctor about some nosedrops to use before a feed to clear the airways. It is important not to let your baby get dehydrated by missing feeds or cutting them short while he has a cold.

Q: We have been sterilizing anything that might go in our baby's mouth, such as rattles and teething rings. When is it safe to stop sterilizing?

A: Most household germs will not make your baby ill, and in fact she was born with some immunities to the germs which are around you all the time. The more dangerous germs are in warm, damp places and in food, which is why sterilizing feeds and feeding equipment is important. With other items ordinary cleanliness is enough – if a rattle is dropped on the floor a good wash with soap and hot water will do. Sterilizing everything she contacts will only delay your baby developing her own immunities.

APPENDIX

The following organizations offer support and information to parents. *The Directory of British Organizations* (ask at your local library) lists many more groups by subject. Voluntary organizations want their services to be used so do not hesitate to contact them. Many operate nationwide and can put you in touch with your nearest branch, but some are small initiatives run by individuals who give what help they can. Often their services have to be fitted around family demands, so please offer to phone back at a convenient time and enclose a stamped addressed envelope if requesting information.

Action Against Allergy, 24–26 George High Street, Hampton Hill, Middlesex TW12 1PD
Action for Sick Children, 300 Kingston Road, London SW20 8LX (020 8542 4848; Helpline: 0800 074 4519). Website: www.actionforsickchildren.org.uk
Association for All Speech-Impaired Children (AFASIC), 69–85 Old Street, London EC1V 9HX (020 7841 8900; Helpline: 0845 355 5577). Website: www.afasic.org.uk. Email: info@afasic.org.uk
Association for Post-Natal Illness, 25 Jerdan Place, Fulham, London SW6 1BE (020 7386 0868)
Association of Breastfeeding Mothers (ABM), PO Box 207, Bridgwater, Somerset TA6 7YT (020 7813 1481). Recorded list of breastfeeding counsellors throughout the UK.
BLISS The National Charity for the New Born, 2nd Floor, Camelford House, 87–89 Albert Embankment, London SE1 7TP (020 7820 9471; Helpline: 0500 618140). Website: www.bliss.org.uk. Email: information@bliss.org.uk. Support for parents of babies who are premature or need special or intensive care.
British Homoeopathic Association, 27a Devonshire Street, London W1N 1RJ (020 7935 2163). Website: www.nhsconfed.net.bha
Child Accident Prevention Trust, 4th Floor, Clerks Court, 18–20 Farringdon Lane, London EC1R 3HA (020 7608 3828). Website: www.capt.org.uk. Email: safe@capt.org.uk
Compassionate Friends, 53 North Street, Bedminster, Bristol BS3 1EN (0117 966 5202; Helpline: 0117 953 9639). Website: www.tfc.org.uk. Email: info@tfc.org.uk. Nationwide organization of bereaved parents offering friendship and emotional support to other bereaved parents.
Contact a Family, 170 Tottenham Court Road, London W1P 0HA (020 7383 3555). Website: www.cafamily.org.uk. Email: info@cafamily.org.uk. Directory of rare conditions and their support networks. Factsheets, parents' guides and telephone helpline.
CRY-SIS, London WC1N 3XX (Helpline: 020 7404 5011, 8am–11pm). Parents with a sleepless or excessively crying baby can be put in touch with a telephone volunteer who has experienced a similar problem.
Down's Syndrome Association, 155 Mitcham Road, London SW17 9PG (020 8682 4001). Website: www.dsa-uk.com
Family Info Link, (0161 477 0606). Website: www.childcarelink.gov.uk/stockport. Email: info@familyinfolink.ssnet.co.uk. Offers free, friendly and confidential information on all aspects of parenting.
Foundation for the Study of Infant Deaths (FSID), Artillery House, 11–19 Artillery Row, London SW1P 1RT (020 7222 8001; Helpline: 020 7233 2090, 24 hours). Website: www.sids.org.uk/fsid. Email: fsid@sids.org.uk. Information, advice, support and individual

befriending for parents coping with a sudden infant death.

Gingerbread, 1st Floor, 7 Sovereign Close, Sovereign Court, London E1W 3HW (0800 018 4218). Website: www.gingerbread.org.uk. Support for lone parents via a network of self-help groups; advice on holidays, legal and welfare rights.

Hyperactive Children's Support Group, Mayfield House, Yapton Road, Barnham, West Sussex PO22 0BJ (01903-725182)

Institute for Complementary Medicine, P O Box 194, London SE16 1QZ (020 7237 5165). Email: icm@icmedicine.co.uk

Invalid Children's Aid Nationwide (ICAN), 4 Dyer's Buildings, Holborn, London EC1N 2JT (0870 010 4066)

La Leche League (Great Britain) BM 3424, London WC1N 3XX (020 7242 1278, 24 hours). Breastfeeding information and support through local groups and telephone counselling.

Meet a Mum Association (MAMA), c/o 58 Madden Avenue, London SE25 4HS (020 8665 0357). Website: www.mama.org.uk. Postnatal support groups and mother-to-mother support for women suffering from postnatal depression.

National Asthma Campaign, Providence House, Providence Place, London N1 0NT (020 7226 2260; Helpline: 08457 010203). Website: www.asthma.org.uk

National Childbirth Trust, Alexandra House, Oldham Terrace, London W3 6NH (020 8992 8637, weekdays 9.30am–4.30pm). Website: www.net-online.org.uk. Antenatal classes, postnatal support, breastfeeding counselling, information, study days, leaflets and merchandise. Branches nationwide.

National Deaf Children's Society, 15 Dufferin Street, London EC1V 8UR (Helpline: 020 7250 0123). Email: fundraising@ndcs.org.uk

National Stepfamily Association, 72 Willesden Lane, London NW6 7TA (020 7372 0844). Advice on issues affecting stepfamilies.

New Ways to Work, 309 Upper Street, London N1 2TY (020 7226 4026). Information and advice about job sharing and flexible working patterns for individuals and employers.

Parentline Plus, (Helpline: 0808 800 2222). Website: www.parentline.co.uk. Offers help and advice on all areas of parenthood.

Parents at Work, 77 Holloway Road, London N7 8JZ (020 7700 5771). Practical advice and support groups on childcare and work-related issues.

Play Matters (National Association of Toy and Leisure Libraries), 68 Churchway, London NW1 1LT (020 7387 9592). Website: www.charitynet.org/~NATLL

Royal Society for Mentally Handicapped Children and Adults (MENCAP), 117–123 Golden Lane, London EC1Y 0RT (020 7454 0454)

Stillbirth and Neonatal Death Society (SANDS), 28 Portland Place, London W1N 4DE (020 7436 5881, Mon, Tues, Wed 10am–3pm). Self help groups and befriending after pregnancy loss, stillbirth or neonatal death; booklet: 'Saying Goodbye to Your Baby'.

Twins and Multiple Births Association (TAMBA), 309 Chester Road, Little Sutton, Ellesmere Port CH66 1QQ. (Twinline: 0173 286 8000, weekdays 6–11pm; weekends 10am–11pm). Website: www.tamba.org.uk. Local clubs and specialist support for families with twins, triplets or more.

Vegan Society, 7 Battle Road, St Leonards-on-Sea, East Sussex TN37 7AA (01424 427393). Website: www.vegansociety.com. Email: info@vegansociety.com

Vegetarian Society of the UK, Parkdale, Dunham Road, Altrincham, Cheshire WA14 4QG (0161 928 0793). Email: bron@vegsoc.org.uk

INDEX

ACKNOWLEDGEMENTS

Special Photography: **Sandra Lousada**
Stylist: **Sheila Birkenshaw**
Illustrations: **Dawn Gunby**

PICTURE CREDITS

ANGELA HAMPTON - FAMILY LIFE PICTURES 6, 36, 39, 99, 104, 106, 111, 112, 113, 118, 129, 143, 146, 156, 160, 163, 167, 175, 183 left
BUBBLES Jacqui Farrow 182, Geoff du Feu 177, Julie Fisher 140, S. Price 151, Loisjoy Thurston 61, 69, 139, Ian West 78, 92, Jennie Woodcock 116
CHILD GROWTH FOUNDATION 124 © 1996 Child Growth Foundation; growth charts reproduced with the kind permission of the Child Growth Foundation, 2 Mayfield Avenue, London W4 1PW
COLLECTIONS Sandra Lousada 10, 123, 130, 164, Anthea Sieveking 4, 7, 27, 52, 91, 132, 170
SALLY AND RICHARD GREENHILL 42, 64
IMAGE BANK Jeff Hunter 76, F. St. C. Renard 125
SANDRA LOUSADA 2, 8/9, 20/21, 48/49, 66/67, 81, 84/85, 96/97, 108/109, 120, 136/137, 149, 153, 158/159, 166, 169, 172/173
LUPE CUNHA 115
MOTHER AND BABY PICTURE LIBRARY Paul Mitchell 82, 87, Ian Boddy 89
REFLECTIONS PHOTO LIBRARY Jennie Woodcock 13, 14, 51, 75, 101, 126, 127, 155, 183 right
TONY STONE IMAGES Bruce Ayres 6/7, 12, Christopher Bissell 13, Ken Fisher 11, Rosanne Olson 103, Terry Vine 5

The publishers would like to thank the parents and babies who kindly modelled for this book.

The information on First Aid contained in this book has been validated by the British Red Cross. This information should not be considered a substitute for proper training. If you wish to take a British Red Cross First Aid Training course then you can contact your local branch or centre of the British Red Cross, which can be found in the telephone directory under 'B'. Information on First Aid training can also be found on the British Red Cross website www.redcross.org.uk